MW00354543

Playbuilding Shakespeare

Wendy Michaels

PUBLISHED BY THE PRESS SYNDICATE OF THE UNIVERSITY OF CAMBRIDGE
The Pitt Building, Trumpington Street, Cambridge CB2 1RP, United Kingdom
CAMBRIDGE UNIVERSITY PRESS
The Edinburgh Building, Cambridge CB2 2RU, United Kingdom
40 West 20th Street, New York, NY 10011–4211, USA
10 Stamford Road, Oakleigh, Melbourne 3166, Australia

© Cambridge University Press 1996
This book is in copyright. Subject to statutory exception and to the provisions of relevant
collective licensing agreeements, no reproduction of any part may take place without the
written permission of Cambridge University Press.

First published 1996
Printed in Australia by Griffin Press
Typeset in 10/12pt Sabon
Designed by Judith Summerfeldt
Illustrations by John Ward

National Library of Australia cataloguing in publication data

Michaels, Wendy.
Playbuilding Shakespeare.
ISBN 0 521 57025 5.
1. Shakespeare, William, 1564-1616 — Juvenile literature.
2. Improvisation (Acting) — Juvenile literature. I. Title.
822.33

Library of Congress cataloguing in publication data

Michaels, Wendy.
Playbuilding Shakespeare/Wendy Michaels.
p. cm.
Summary: Explores five of Shakespeare's plays as performance pieces by using techniques
which draw on aspects of playbuilding: plays included are: "A Midsummer Night's Dream",
"The Merchant of Venice", "Julius Caesar", "Romeo and Juliet", and "Macbeth".
ISBN 0-521-57025-5
1. Shakespeare, William, 1564-1616 — Dramatic production — Problems,
exercises, etc. — Juvenile literature. 2. Shakespeare, William,
1564-1616 — Stage history — Problems, exercises, etc. — Juevenile
literature. 3. Improvisation (Acting) —Problems, exercises, etc. — Juvenile literature. [1.
Shakespeare, William, 1564-1616 — Dramatic production. 2. Shakespeare, William, 1564-
1616 — Stage history. 3. Plays—Improvisation.] I. Title.
PR3091.M53 1996
822.3'3 — dc20
                                                                        96-15738
                                                                              CIP
                                                                               AC

A catalogue record for this book is available from the British Library

ISBN 0 521 57025 5 paperback

Notice to Teachers
The contents of this book are in the copyright of Cambridge University Press. Unauthorised
copying of any of these pages is illegal and detrimental to the interests of authors.

For authorised copying within Australia please check that your institution has a licence from
Copyright Agency Limited. This permits the copying of small parts of the text, in limited
quantities, within the conditions set out in the Licence.

Table of Contents

For Sage and Phoebe
may their experiences of the Bard be joyful explorations

Acknowledgements

I wish to acknowledge the inspiration of Louis Fantasia, and the on-going support of Nick Shimmin, Tanya Dalgleish, Donna Gibbs and my three sons, Evan, Owen and Selwyn.

Prologue

The name of Shakespeare evokes different responses from different people. For some, he is the greatest writer in the English language. For others, he brings back memories of English classes where the meaning of the works was clouded by language that often didn't seem to make sense and by endless translations into 'modern English'. And for others, he is the source and inspiration of some of the most exciting and exhilarating experiences in the theatre and cinema.

Shakespeare's plays were written for the stage. Indeed, they were first and foremost scripts for performances. It was only later that they were written down, published, and read as literature. And it was long, long after Shakespeare's death that they began to be studied in schools.

Unfortunately, perhaps, study of the plays in schools has often been divorced from their lives on stages. Those who studied Shakespeare's plays as pieces of literature, while experiencing the richness of the language, all too often missed out on the richness of the drama and theatre.

For a long period of time, the performances of the plays on the stage occurred on proscenium arch stages – quite a different stage configuration from the one that Shakespeare used. Thus, those who tried to work with stage performances of the plays were not really getting to the heart of the plays which Shakespeare wrote for the large thrust stages of the Elizabethan theatres.

But all this is beginning to change. The rebuilding of the Globe Theatre in London is challenging theatre practitioners and theatre educators to look at the plays in a different way. Film versions of the plays are reawakening an interest in the stories and modern productions are finding a style of acting that better suits the poetic drama that Shakespeare wrote.

This book is designed to allow students to explore aspects of five of Shakespeare's plays as performance pieces. The techniques used in the book draw on aspects of playbuilding. At the end of each unit, students should be able to present a version of Shakespeare's play, drawing on their own improvised work as well as drawing on the work of Shakespeare himself. There are Cambridge School Shakespeare editions of each of the plays, which provide further suggestions for workshop activities.

This book gives students licence to play with the plays in the way that real actors, directors and dramaturges do in the theatre.

Playbuilding

Playbuilding is a way of working in drama which has rich possibilities for learning. Playbuilding involves groups of students working collaboratively to create a play. The play may be developed from ideas or issues, from characters or from already known stories. (Shakespeare himself used well-known stories as the basis of his plays.) Playbuilding does not usually begin with a complete script for performance, but rather with the ideas, issues, characters or story. The playbuilt play is developed from the fragments of ideas, issues, characters and stories that are explored in the collaborative workshop process.

Playbuilding requires a workshop approach to the development of the play. It engages groups in exploring, through a range of improvisation techniques, scenes which may be included in the final performed play. While there may be a dramaturge who assists in the development of the final script, the process differs from scripted theatre in that the script emerges through the workshop activities. In some cases the 'script' may be recorded in full, while in others it may only be recorded as a running order, with individual scenes identified through description of the scenario rather than as complete dialogue and action.

Because playbuilding does not begin with a script, but with a workshop approach, the role of the director differs from that used in rehearsing a scripted play. At the beginning of the work, no one knows what the final play will look like. Some scenes that are developed during the playbuilding process may be excluded from the final product. The order of the scenes may not be decided until near the end of the process. The ways of linking the scenes may only be decided towards the end of the process. The director is, therefore, working as part of the creative collaborative process, rather than as an interpreter of an already completed script.

Playbuilt plays tend to be very fluid. They tend to consist of collage or anthology formats with short scenes, drawing on moments of tableau, freeze framing, double scenes with intercut lines, use of aside, monologue and soliloquy and so on. This structure and format makes them particularly suited to the classroom.

Playbuilt plays work best on open stages with minimal use of furniture and props. In this sense they are very like the plays that Shakespeare himself wrote. His plays, not surprisingly, lend themselves well to this style of exploration.

The narrative structures used in playbuilt plays can vary. There may be a single storyline with the events related in chronological order. There may also be use of flashbacks that show events of a previous time and their effects on present events. There may be a leap forward in time so that the playing time does not evenly represent the real time of the events being played. There is often also a use of dual time sequences to show simultaneous action. There may also be more complex storylines with interweaving plots.

Playbuilt plays do not generally make use of a narrator. They present multiple viewpoints through allowing characters to speak to each other as well as directly to the audience.

The use of a range of improvisation techniques is central to the playbuilding process. This does not mean simply 'making it up as you go along'. Improvisation can be very fluid and exploratory in this sense, but it can also be highly structured, drawing on a range of dramatic forms. Both types of improvisation are used in this book.

Playbuilding is a group process that relies upon fluid roles and relationships. While some members of the groups may take particular responsibility for a particular role within the group or a particular role within the play, the group process provides opportunities for others to step into and out of the same role at different points, even during the final presentation.

Playbuilding is also about hard work. It requires rigorous thinking and active engagement with ideas and how these ideas can be presented in dramatic forms. Throughout the process of building the play, the group needs to be constantly asking two questions:

- *What* ideas do we want to communicate to the audience?
- *How* can we communicate these ideas through the dramatic form?

There is a wide range of strategies to be used in playbuilding. Many of these are used in the chapters in this book.

There are many different starting points for playbuilding. These include approaches which begin with stories, or with characters, or with settings, or with issues and ideas. In this book the emphasis is primarily on playbuilding from the stories, characters and issues of some of Shakespeare's plays.

Trippingly on the Tongue

The Language of Shakespeare's Stage

The language of Shakespeare's plays is sometimes daunting when you first encounter it. Although it may appear ancient at times, it is not old English – in fact it is usually referred to as the beginning of modern English. The difficulty with the language arises partly because Shakespeare uses some words which we no longer use today, and other words now have different meanings. It also seems difficult because it is verse drama – something that we are not so accustomed to today. It is the verse drama, in fact, which gives the language its richness and complexity.

Within the poetry of each play, Shakespeare crafted wonderful images, many of which arose from the plethora of poetic devices which he used to effect. On his stage they were particularly effective because his 'players' understood the rhetorical devices and were trained to render them through voice, gestures and movement.

Shakespeare wrote not only in verse. He used three main types of language forms. First, he used prose, which is the language of everyday speech.

> They met me in the day of success, and I have learned by the perfectest report they have more in them than mortal knowledge. When I burned in desire to question them further, they made themselves air, into which they vanished.

Secondly, he used rhyming verse, which is something which we are used to from our acquaintance with poetry. Sometimes he used rhyming verse, where alternate lines rhymed, and at other times he used rhyming couplets.

The ousel cock so black of hue,
    With orange-tawny bill,
The throstle with his note so true,
    The wren with little quill –
The finch, the sparrow, and the lark,
    The plainsong cuckoo grey,
Whose note full many a man doth mark
    And dares not answer nay.

I do wander everywhere
Swifter than the moon's sphere;
And I serve the Fairy Queen,
To dew her orbs upon the green.

Thirdly, and most commonly, he used a verse form called 'blank verse'. This verse form consists of unrhymed lines which have ten syllables in each line, commonly in the metrical pattern of unstressed syllable followed by stressed syllable.

For them, the gracious Duncan have I murdered,
Put rancours in the vessel of my peace
Only for them, and mine eternal jewel
Given to the common enemy of man,
To make them kings, the seeds of Banquo kings.

Shakespeare varied this pattern at times, of course, and when he did vary it, it was for a particular purpose, usually to mark a change of direction or mood, or for particular emphasis.

                              I'll go no more.
I am afraid to think what I have done;
Look on't again, I dare not.

You may wish to work through some of the following activities which explore Shakespeare's writing before you begin the playbuilding section of this book.

✻ *Sound sense*

We shall begin with Shakespeare's use of the sounds of English. Basically there are two broad types of sounds in English – vowels and consonants. Vowel sounds are those voiced sounds which are not impeded or blocked in the mouth, but are shaped, primarily by the lips. Consonants are those voiced and voiceless sounds which are impeded or blocked in the mouth by some of the organs of articulation: the tongue, teeth, lips, hard and soft palate.

Vowels

The vowel sounds tend to provide the emotional component of the meaning while the consonant sounds tend to contribute to the rhythmic qualities.

The vowel sounds can be identified in terms of their length. They can also be identified according to the shape of the mouth as they are made. They are all voiced sounds.

Activity

Work with a partner. Say each of the following vowel sounds to each other, repeating the sounds a number of times. Listen for the length of the sound and watch how the lips shape the sound. What kinds of feelings or moods are associated with each sound?

The short vowel sounds comprise:

i	bit
e	bet
a	bat
er	butt<u>er</u>
u	but
o	bottle
oo	boot

The long vowels comprise:

EE	thee
ER	her
AH	far
AW	sword
OO	moon

The longest of the vowel sounds are the diphthongs and triphthongs. They comprise:

OH	show
AIR	fair
EAR	fear
IRE	sire
OUR	hour

Activity

The following verses come from Shakespeare's poem, *Venus and Adonis*. Work with a partner. Take turns to read each stanza aloud. Stress the vowel sounds and explore the moods that they suggest.

Even as the sun with purple-coloured face
Had tane his last leave of the weeping morn,
Rose-cheeked Adonis hied him to the chase;
Hunting he loved, but love he laughed to scorn.
   Sick-thoughted Venus makes amain unto him,
   And like a bold-faced suitor gins to woo him.

With this she seizeth on his sweating palm,
The precedent of pith and livelihood,
And trembling in her passion calls it balm,
Earth's sovereign salve to do a goddess good.
   Being so enraged, desire doth lend her force
   Courageously to pluck him from his horse.

So soon was she along as he was down,
Each leaning on their elbows and their hips;
Now doth she stroke his cheek, now doth he frown
And gins to chide, but soon she stops his lips,
   And kissing speaks, with lustful language broken,
   'If thou wilt chide, thy lips shall never open.'

Forced to content, but never to obey,
Panting he lies and breatheth in her face.
She feedeth on the steam as on a prey,
And calls it heavenly moisture, air of grace,
   Wishing her cheeks were gardens full of flowers,
   So they were dewed with such distilling showers.

Activity

Much of the lyrical beauty of the following edited speech from *The Merchant of Venice* comes from the play of the vowel sounds. Work with a partner. Read these lines and explore the sounds and cadences of the speech. How do the vowel sounds help to establish the romantic mood?

LORENZO   How sweet the moonlight sleeps upon this bank!
              Here will we sit, and let the sounds of music
              Creep in our ears; soft stillness and the night
              Become the touches of sweet harmony.
              Sit, Jessica. Look how the floor of heaven
              Is thick inlaid with patens of bright gold.
              There's not the smallest orb which thou behold'st
              But in his motion like an angel sings,
              Still choiring to the young-eyed cherubins.
              Such harmony is in immortal souls,
              But whilst this muddy vesture of decay

Doth grossly close it in, we cannot hear it.
Come, ho! and wake Diana with a hymn.
With sweetest touches pierce your mistress' ear,
And draw her home with music.

Consonants

The consonant sounds can be classified according to how they are made. The main classifications based on how these sounds are made include: plosives, fricatives, affricatives, sibilants, laterals, nasals and the aspirate. They can be voiced or voiceless.

The **plosive sounds** are made by the voice or breath being held back momentarily at different points by the tongue, teeth, palate or lips, and then exploding from the mouth. They consist of:

p   Puck

b   Bottom

t   tyrant

d   Demetrius

k   king

g   gallop

Activity

Experiment with these sounds and then say the following lines stressing the sounds in the words to create the rhythmic pattern.

Double, double toil and trouble
Fire burn, and cauldron bubble.

A drum, a drum;
Macbeth doth come.

The **fricative sounds** are made by the voice or breath being partially blocked. There is a friction in the mouth as the breath or voice escapes through the partial blockage. They consist of:

f   Flute

v   vanquish

th   Thisbe

th   thus

Activity

Experiment with these sounds and then say the following lines stressing the sounds in the words to create the rhythmic pattern.

Full fathom five
Thy father lies.

So foul and fair a day I have not seen.

The **affricative sounds** are a combination of the plosive and fricative sounds. They are made by a partial blockage followed by an explosion. They include:

tch   church

j   judge

Activity

Experiment with these sounds and then say the following lines stressing the sounds in the words to create the rhythmic pattern.

I am dying, Egypt, dying.

Be innocent of the knowledge, dearest chuck.

The **sibilant sounds** are made by the breath or voice slipping over the side of the tongue to escape from the mouth. They include:

s   so

z   zounds

sh   show

s/z   measure

Activity

Experiment with these sounds and then say the following lines stressing the sounds in the words to create the rhythmic pattern.

Show his eyes and grieve his heart,
Come like shadows, so depart.

measure for measure

The **lateral sounds** also allow the sound to slide over the edge of the tongue in a lilting fashion. They include:

l   lizard

r   ronyon

Activity

Experiment with these sounds and then say the following line stressing the sounds in the words to create the rhythmic pattern.

Lizard's leg, and howlet's wing.

The **nasal sounds** are made when the soft palate is raised so that the sound is unable to enter and resonate in the nasal chamber. They include:

n   nuts

m   munch

ng   sing

Activity

Experiment with these sounds and then say the following lines stressing the sounds in the words to create the rhythmic pattern.

A sailor's wife had chestnuts in her lap
And munched, and munched, and munched.

The **aspirate sound** is a breathed sound that escapes through the open mouth. It is:

h   howlet

Activity

Experiment with this sound and then say the following line stressing the sounds in the words to create the rhythmic pattern.

What hempen homespuns have we swaggering here.

✳ *Sound patterning*

The virtue in Shakespeare's craft derives from the sound patterning of the words in the lines and throughout the verse. This includes the obvious patterns of rhyme and near rhyme as well as the patterns associated with repetition of vowel sounds (assonance) and consonant sounds (alliteration).

Activity

Work with a partner. Read the following stanzas from *The Passionate Pilgrim* to each other. Explore the sound patterns that produce the rhyme in this verse.

> If music and sweet poetry agree,
> As they must needs, the sister and the brother,
> Then must the love be great 'twixt thee and me,
> Because thou lov'st the one, and I the other.
> Dowland to thee is dear, whose heavenly touch
> Upon the lute doth ravish human sense;
> Spenser to me, whose deep conceit is such
> As passing all conceit needs no defence.
> Thou lov'st to hear the sweet melodious sound
> That Phoebus' lute, the queen of music, makes;
> And I in deep delight am chiefly drowned
> When as himself to singing he betakes.
> One god is god of both, as poets feign;
> One knight loves both, and both in thee remain.

Activity

Work with a partner. Read the following lines and explore the sounds of the near rhyme in this verse from *The Passionate Pilgrim*. Notice that the vowel sounds change slightly to produce the near rhyme.

> If love made me forsworn, how shall I swear to love?
> O never faith could hold, if not to beauty vowed.
> Though to myself forsworn, to thee I'll constant prove;
> Those thoughts to me like oaks, to thee like osiers bowed.

✳ *Blank verse*

Most of Shakespeare's plays are written in blank verse (unrhymed iambic pentameter). There are, of course, variations to the pattern of the blank verse and at times the sense of the lines even seems to work against the metre. However, more often the sense of the line, its full force and effect, comes from the metrical pattern in the line.

Activity

Experiment with reading the following lines so that you feel their metrical pattern (iambic pentameter) and uncover their meaning.

A fool/ish thought /to say /a sor/ry sight/

A lit/tle wa/ter clears/ us of/ this deed/

I con/jure you /by that /which you /profess/

Iambic pentameter renders the last syllable in the line of verse a stressed syllable. It is important that the force of this last syllable is not lost by dropping the voice.

Activity

Work with a partner. Experiment with reading these lines aloud and listen for the stress on the last syllable.

When shall we three meet *again*?

The instruments of darkness tell us *truths*.

But screw your courage to the sticking *place*.

That which hath made them drunk hath made me *bold*.

What hath quenched them hath given me *fire*.

Why did you bring these daggers from the *place*?

When the metrical pattern is varied it is usually to point to some aspect of the meaning. For instance, in the following activity the last foot of the line has two stressed syllables (Spondee foot).

Activity

Experiment with reading this line with the stress on both of the last syllables. How does this affect the meaning?

Tongue nor heart cannot conceive nor *name thee*!

✳ Prosodic devices

Caesura

Shakespeare also makes use of the device known as 'caesura'. This is literally a 'cut' in the line of verse. It is usually signalled by punctuation such as a full stop or comma. While the caesura allows the opportunity for a breath pause, it has a more important function in the line and that is to juxtapose the idea enunciated immediately before the caesura with the idea posited at the end of the line. This juxtaposition serves either to compare or to contrast these ideas or images.

Activity

Work with a partner and experiment with some of the following lines which use caesura. Listen for the way that the two ideas are balanced and contrasted through the juxtaposition established by the caesura.

Why did he marry *Fulvia*, / and not love *her*?

There's a great spirit *gone*! / Thus did I desire *it*.

I have no power upon *you*: / hers you *are*.

I'll frown and be *perverse*, / and say thee *nay*.

Hie you to *church* / I must another *way*

If all else *fayself* have power to *die*

Enjambment

Allied to the use of caesura is the use of enjambment, or run-on lines. A run-on line or enjambed line is one where the sense of the line runs on to the next line with no punctuation at the end of the line. If this type of line is spoken with a pause at the end it is likely to interrupt the sense. If it is spoken without any metrical adjustment, the rhythm of the verse is interrupted. What is needed here is a 'suspensive pause'. This means that the last stressed syllable is slightly elongated before the voice moves on to the next line.

Activity

Experiment with the following lines. First read them stopping at the end of the line and then moving to the next line. Then try reading them as prose, with no stopping or adjustment to the rhythm of the verse. Then read them using a 'suspensive pause', i.e. elongating the last stressed syllable before moving on to the next line.

> From forth the fatal loins of these two foes
> A pair of star-crossed lovers take their life.

> Here were the servants of your adversary
> And yours, close fighting ere I did approach.

> Towards him I made, but he was ware of me
> And stole into the covert of the wood.

> He that is strucken blind cannot forget
> The precious treasure of his eyesight lost.

> But no more deep will I endart mine eye
> Than your consent gives strength to make it fly.

> My lips, two blushing pilgrims, ready stand
> To smooth that rough touch with a tender kiss.

> But trust me, gentleman, I'll prove more true
> Than those that have more cunning to be strange.

> But my true love is grown to such excess
> I cannot sum up sum of half my wealth.

> For thou wilt lie upon the wings of night
> Whiter than new snow upon a raven's back.

> Thy tears are womanish, thy wild acts denote
> The unreasonable fury of a beast.

Verse lining

Shakespeare at times has two characters share the same line of verse. This is known as verse lining. To keep the rhythm of the verse, the characters must treat their lines as if they are one. There needs to be no break between the speeches.

Activity

Work with a partner and experiment with saying these lines. First read them with a pause in between each of the speakers, then read them sharing the rhythm of the verse. Make sure that there is no pause or break between the two speakers who are sharing this single line of verse.

MACBETH	Your children shall be kings. /
BANQUO	You shall be king.

MACBETH	My dearest love,
	Duncan comes here tonight. /
LADY MACBETH	And when goes hence?
MACBETH	Tomorrow as he purposes. /
LADY MACBETH	O never
	Shall sun that morrow see.

MACBETH	Hath he asked for me? /
LADY MACBETH	Know you not he has?

LADY MACBETH	Did you not speak? /
MACBETH	When? /
LADY MACBETH	Now. /
MACBETH	As I descended? /
LADY MACBETH	Ay.

Prose

Shakespeare also used prose, and his prose has very different textures and patterns and rhythms to his verse. The rhythm of the prose is closely tied to the syntax of the prose.

Activity

Experiment with the rhythm of the following speech of Casca's from *Julius Caesar*, noting the markers which indicate the syntactical units. Notice how the rhythm speeds up and slows down at different points. Notice how this change of pace creates the dramatic effect of the speech.

I can as well be hanged as tell the manner of it. / It was mere foolery, / I did not mark it. / I saw Mark Antony offer him a crown – / yet 'twas not a crown neither, / 'twas one of these coronets – / and, / as I told you,/ he put it by once; / but for all that, / to my thinking / he would fain have had it. / Then he offered it to him again; / then he put it by again; / but to my thinking / he was very loath to lay his fingers off it. / And then he offered it the third time; / he put it the third time by, / and still as he refused it, / the rabblement hooted, / and clapped their chopped hands, / and threw up their sweaty nightcaps, / and uttered such a deal of stinking breath because Caesar refused the crown / that it had, almost, choked Caesar, / for he swounded / and fell down at it.

✴ *Rhetorical devices*

The intricate thought patterns in Shakespeare's works are revealed through the patterns of language and particularly through the use of rhetorical devices. The Elizabethan audiences were probably more familiar with these than modern audiences are likely to be. Nevertheless, the role of the actor or player is to make these thought patterns explicit through the speaking of the lines.

Antithesis

A common device employed by Shakespeare is antithesis. Antithesis means opposition. By juxtaposing opposite ideas, images and sound and rhythm patterns, meaning is clarified.

Sometimes the antithetical ideas and images are placed in close proximity to each other. A further device which Shakespeare uses is oxymoron. Here two antithetical ideas are placed together in close proximity – 'parting is such *sweet sorrow*'.

Activity

Work with a partner. Read these lines aloud, stressing the opposite ideas in the lines. Notice how sound patterns assist you to create the opposition of ideas.

So *foul* and *fair* a day I have not seen.

Fair is *foul*, and *foul* is *fair*.

The *day* to *cheer*, and *night*'s dank dew to *dry*.

The earth that's nature's *mother* is her *tomb*;
What is her burying *grave*, that is her *womb*.

It was the *nightingale*, and not the *lark*.

More *light* and *light*, more *dark* and *dark* our woes!

At other times the antithetical words will be separated out in the speeches or even across speeches. Sometimes a character may respond to another by setting his or her speech in opposition to the other.

Activity

Work with a partner. Read the following speeches and explore the ways that they work in opposition to one another.

FRIAR LAWRENCE   So smile the heavens upon this holy act,
                   That after-hours with sorrow chide us not.

ROMEO   Amen, amen! but come what sorrow can,
                   It cannot countervail the exchange of joy
                   That one short minute gives me in her sight.

ROMEO   Ah, Juliet, if the measure of thy joy
                   Be heaped like mine, and that thy skill be more
                   To blazon it, then sweeten with thy breath
                   This neighbour air, and let rich music's tongue
                   Unfold the imagined happiness that both
                   Receive in either by this dear encounter.

JULIET   Conceit, more rich in matter than in words,
                   Brags of his substance, not of ornament;
                   They are but beggars that can count their worth,
                   But my true love is grown to such excess
                   I cannot sum up sum of half my wealth.

Pun

A common device employed by Shakespeare is the pun or play on words. Contemporary audiences delight in such word games. To appreciate some of the word games in Shakespeare's plays, however, it is necessary to know the kinds of connotations that particular words had in Shakespeare's time. Footnotes to the Cambridge School Shakespeare editions of the texts usually provide you with the information that will help you to make sense of the puns.

Repetition

Repetition of words and phrases is another common device that Shakespeare employs to make a point. It is important to look for patterns of repetition, as they point to the key ideas which Shakespeare is underlining. Sometimes the repetition builds up a kind of climax, and you feel you are climbing a metaphorical ladder.

Activity

Work with a partner. Experiment with this passage, noting how the repetition and antithesis build up to the climax of the speech. Trace the words which help create the 'ladder' that leads to the climax.

RICHARD II   I have been studying how I may compare
This prison where I live unto the world,
And for because the world is populous
And here is not a creature but myself
I cannot do it. Yet I'll hammer't out.
My brain I'll prove the female to my soul,
My soul the father, and these two beget
A generation of still breeding thoughts,
And these same thoughts people this little world.
In humours like the people of this world,
For no thought is contented. The better sort,
As thoughts of things divine, are intermixed
With scruples, and do set the word itself
Against the word.

❈ *Dramatically speaking*

Shakespeare's plays are exciting because of their dramatic and theatrical form. The nature of the theatre and the stage resulted in plays which allowed the actors and audience to interact in various ways.

Shakespeare's theatre was a round-shaped building, open to the elements. The wooden building had a large thrust stage, with the audience either seated in the galleries or standing in the pit on three sides of the stage. The stage had a roof over it, often referred to as the Heavens, as did the galleries, but there was no roof over the pit where the 'groundlings' gathered. There were only two doors for entrances on to the stage. There was no scenery, few props and little furniture used on the stage.

The plays were performed without an interval, and without breaks in between scenes. This made the action swift and the plays very fluid and gave the impression of watching a kaleidoscope of action. Time and place were not particularly significant. Many of the scenes could have occurred anywhere. When Shakespeare wanted to locate action in a particular place or in a particular time, he incorporated this information in the actors' lines.

The size and shape of Shakespeare's stage lent itself to a wide range of different types of actions. Fights, battles, balls, processions, chases, murders, as well as intimate love scenes and eavesdropping scenes were all possible on this stage.

Importantly, the stage allowed for different types of speeches. The characters could talk not only to each other in different ways but also to the audience. Shakespeare used dialogue, monologue and duologue, as well as aside and soliloquy.

Dialogue

Dialogue involved a number of characters interacting with each other in the scene. Work with a small group and read the following lines, making it sound like a conversation.

QUINCE   What sayest thou, bully Bottom?

BOTTOM   There are things in this comedy of Pyramus and Thisbe that will never please. First, Pyramus must draw a sword to kill himself, which the ladies cannot abide. How answer you that?

SNOUT   By'r lakin, a parlous fear!

STARVELING   I believe we must leave the killing out, when all is done.

Monologue

Monologue involved a character in making a long uninterrupted speech to a group of characters in the scene. Work with a partner. One should read the speech below. Notice what the listener does during this speech.

PUCK   My mistress with a monster is in love.
Near to her close and consecrated bower,
While she was in her dull and sleeping hour,
A crew of patches, rude mechanicals,
That work for bread upon Athenian stalls,
Were met together to rehearse a play
Intended for great Theseus' nuptial day.
The shallowest thick-skin of that barren sort,
Who Pyramus presented, in their sport
Forsook his scene and entered in a brake,
When I did him this advantage take:
An ass's nole I fixèd on his head.

Duologue

Duologue involved two characters alone on the stage interacting. Work with a partner. Read the following duologue. Notice how the two characters interact.

DEMETRIUS   You spend your passion on a misprised mood.
I am not guilty of Lysander's blood,
Nor is he dead, for aught that I can tell.

HERMIA   I pray thee, tell me then that he is well.

DEMETRIUS   And if I could, what should I get therefor?

HERMIA	A privilege, never to see me more;
	And from thy hated presence part I so.
	See me no more, whether he be dead or no.

Aside

Aside involved a character in a scene speaking directly to the audience, usually commenting on the actions of the characters in the scene. Work in a group. Speak these lines. Notice how the character makes the aside so that the others do not hear it.

CAESAR	I am to blame to be thus waited for.
	Now, Cinna, now, Metellus. What, Trebonius,
	I have an hour's talk in store for you.
	Remember that you call on me today;
	Be near me that I may remember you.
TREBONIUS	Caesar I will. [*Aside*] And so near will I be
	That your best friends shall wish I had been further.

Soliloquy

Soliloquy involved a character alone on the stage speaking directly to the audience, usually confessing his or her inner feelings or thoughts, or trying to justify to the audience some action that he or she has taken or is about to take. Work with a group. One person should read the soliloquy while the others are the audience.

CASSIUS	Well, Brutus, thou art noble; yet I see
	Thy honourable metal may be wrought
	From that it is disposed. Therefore it is meet
	That noble minds keep ever with their likes;
	For who so firm that cannot be seduced?
	Caesar doth bear me hard, but he loves Brutus.
	If I were Brutus now and he were Cassius,
	He should not humour me. I will this night,
	In several hands, in at his windows throw,
	As if they came from several citizens,
	Writings, all tending to the great opinion
	That Rome holds of his name, wherein obscurely
	Caesar's ambition shall be glancèd at.
	And after this let Caesar seat him sure,
	For we will shake him, or worse days endure.

Prologue and epilogue

Shakespeare also prefaced some plays with a prologue and ended some plays with an epilogue. These were spoken either by an anonymous chorus-like character, or by one of the characters in the play. The prologue was used to set the scene, while the epilogue tended to round off and signal the end of the play. Work in groups and experiment with the following prologue and epilogue.

Prologue to *Romeo and Juliet*

CHORUS   Two households, both alike in dignity,
              In fair Verona (where we lay our scene),
              From ancient grudge break to new mutiny,
              Where civil blood makes civil hands unclean.
              From forth the fatal loins of these two foes
              A pair of star-crossed lovers take their life;
              Whose misadventured piteous overthrows
              Doth with their death bury their parents' strife.
              The fearful passage of their death-marked love,
              And the continuance of their parents' rage,
              Which but their children's end nought could remove,
              Is now the two hours' traffic of our stage;
              The which if you with patient ears attend,
              What here shall miss, our toil shall strive to mend.

Epilogue to *A Midsummer Night's Dream*

PUCK   If we shadows have offended,
              Think but this, and all is mended:
              That you have but slumbered here
              While these visions did appear;
              And this weak and idle theme,
              No more yielding but a dream.
              Gentles, do not reprehend;
              If you pardon, we will mend.
              And, as I am an honest Puck,
              If we have unearnèd luck
              Now to 'scape the serpent's tongue
              We will make amends ere long,
              Else the Puck a liar call.
              So, good night unto you all.
              Give me your hands, if we be friends,
              And Robin shall restore amends.

A Lamentable Comedy

2

A Midsummer Night's Dream

In this unit of work you are going to explore a part of *A Midsummer Night's Dream*. The part of the play which you will be exploring is the 'play within the play'. On Shakespeare's stage it was common for a play to happen within the main play. The characters in the main play became part of the audience for the play within the play. The real audience watched the characters watching the main play as well as the play itself. This device allowed Shakespeare to make strong comments about the ideas of the main play itself.

Shakespeare worked in a company of actors or players. All the actors were male, so any female parts in the plays had to be taken by male actors. Usually these parts were played by young boys or the younger men of the company.

The company worked as a collaborative ensemble. The players were all 'sharers' in the company. The parts which actors or players took in the plays were often determined by their physique and by their temperament. Parts were essentially type-cast.

✳ *Preliminary discussion*

Work together in groups of about seven or eight. Talk about the soapies you regularly watch on television. Make a list of the key characters in these soapies. Beside each character write the name of the actor who plays the part, and words to describe the physique and the temperament or personality of

the soapie character. Talk about why the particular actor might suit the particular part that he or she plays. Are there stereotypical characters involved in these programs?

You may wish to research some of the players of Shakespeare's time, such as William Kemp or Richard Burbage. Try to find out what roles these characters played and how the roles suited their physique and temperament.

Record your information in your logbook.

Stock characters

Shakespeare used many of the characters drawn from *commedia dell'arte* in his plays. These characters were stock characters or stereotypes. They had dominant characteristics which were related to their physical appearance. Some of these characters included:

- faithful, poetic lover
- opportunistic intriguer
- miserly old bachelor
- eloquent philosopher
- bombastic braggart
- dull, coarse bumpkin
- trustworthy servant
- simpleton
- noble, innocent woman
- fresh and frisky lass
- garrulous old woman.

Spend time talking in your group about these stock characters or stereotypes. Draw up a chart in which you record the physical and personality characteristics that you would expect for each of these stock characters.

If you had to cast these roles from the soapie actors, who would you select to play each part?

Share your 'castings' with other groups and discuss the impressions you have of these characters.

✻ *Scenarios*

Many of Shakespeare's plays are built up from scenarios that bring some of these stock characters into complicating situations. These complicating situations are usually referred to as scenarios. Two examples follow:

> The faithful, poetic lover, unsuccessfully in love with the noble, innocent woman, has decided to kill himself. He tries several methods and each one fails: the rope breaks; he cuts his finger but it does not bleed fast enough; alcohol makes him happy rather than drugged; when he holds his nose he breathes through his mouth. Finally, he is rescued by the fresh and frisky lass who distracts him from his first love.

> The miserly old bachelor complains of feeling ill in order to avoid paying out money that he owes to his neighbours. The opportunistic intriguer comes disguised as a doctor and carries out some hocus pocus which causes the bachelor to faint. He is then pronounced dead by the disguised doctor. All his neighbours come to the wake. They eat and drink, paying no attention to the corpse. The bachelor comes to life, realises the situation and decides to remain quiet in order to hear what they say about him. He listens to their remarks – none too flattering – about him and watches them consume his wine and feast on his stock of fine food. Then to teach them a lesson, he rises like a ghost and begins to walk among them. They run away in fright.

Work in groups of four or five. Select some of the stock *commedia* characters and write a scenario that shows them in a complicating situation. Your scenario should begin by introducing the characters, then demonstrate the complication and identify how it is resolved. The scenario should demonstrate how the particular physical and temperamental or personality characteristics of the characters contribute to the situation.

Present your scenario to the class in a narrative form, i.e. tell the story of the scenario to the class. Allow others to question aspects of the scenario for clarification.

Write your scenario in your logbook.

✻ *Answer as I call you*

Young boys in Shakespeare's day were apprenticed to adult companies, partly so that there were boys who could play the parts of women, and partly to learn the craft of 'playing'. In medieval times, plays had been performed by the members of guilds, and these plays had travelled from town to town. Shakespeare's company also toured beyond London. In Shakespeare's day, the development of boy companies was seen as a threat to the adult companies because of their popularity.

Players were generally viewed with ambivalence. On the one hand they were applauded for their skill, and on the other hand they were seen as vagrants or vagabonds because of their lifestyle. Nevertheless, performing in a play was seen as a desirable activity.

In *A Midsummer Night's Dream*, Shakespeare shows the desire of some very ordinary tradesmen or Mechanicals to perform a play for the wedding celebrations of Theseus and Hippolyta. Each of these men was identified by name and by his trade. Each is recognisable as one of the *commedia dell'arte* stock characters.

Work in groups of six. Each member of your group is to be cast for a part in a play. The parts will need to be cast on the basis of the physical characteristics and temperamental or personality characteristics of the members of the group.

These are the parts that you will cast:

- leader and organiser – Peter Quince (a carpenter)
- conceited simpleton, energetic, oblivious of others' opinions – Nick Bottom (a weaver)
- hesitant, effeminate man – Francis Flute (a bellows mender)
- quiet, articulate, confident man – Tom Snout (a tinker)
- dull-witted, slow, shy man – Snug (a joiner)
- timid man, terrified of speaking in public – Robin Starveling (a tailor).

Once you have decided who is to be cast as each character, improvise a scene where each character has the opportunity to speak about himself. Record the scene in your logbook.

✄ *May I introduce myself*

You are now going to work to build up the character that you have adopted. Work in six groups. Each group should consist of all the players for one character. All the Quinces should be in one group, all the Bottoms in another group and so on.

In these groups, talk about how you see the character that you are all playing. Talk about the features of his personality. You may wish to make a list of words to describe his personality. You may individually have slightly different views of this character.

Build up the life history of this character. You may need to do some research to find out about his trade. What did a tinker or a bellows mender do? Find out about his apprenticeship and his lifestyle, then develop some of the stories which might be associated with his village life, with his apprenticeship and the craft that he practises. Why do you think he might want to take part in a play that is to be performed at the wedding of Theseus and Hippolyta?

Talk about how he would stand and move. Experiment with different gestures, movements and walks. Talk about how he would speak. Experiment with different voices for the character.

Working together, write a short monologue for this character which could be used to introduce him. Talk about how the character would speak and address his audience.

Work together as a group to rehearse this monologue. Select one person to present the monologue, introducing your character to the other groups.

Spend some time discussing these characters. Record your ideas in your logbook.

✖ *Take pains, be perfect*

Now that you know your character better you are going to allow him to interact with other characters. Work in groups of six so that there is one person playing each of the characters in each of the groups. Each player will stay in the role developed in the last activity, i.e. as Quince, Bottom, Snug etc. Each group is to take the following scenario and develop depictions based on it.

> The six characters, Quince, Bottom, Flute, Snout, Snug and Starveling have agreed to meet in a forest. They have agreed to be part of a festival for the wedding of Theseus and Hippolyta.
>
> Quince tries to organise each character into taking on the particular role for the play that he wants them to perform. He calls out the parts one at a time.
>
> Bottom keeps pushing himself into the limelight. He wants to play the biggest part and be on the stage all the time.
>
> When Quince calls out Flute's part, Bottom says he wants to play it as well as his own. Quince keeps trying to put him in his place without hurting his feelings.
>
> Snug is very nervous. When his part is called out he says he is not confident that he will be able to learn his lines.
>
> When Starveling's part is called he says he wishes he had not agreed to come and he tries to escape from the group.
>
> Quince finally gets them in order and brings them together in a sort of a fashion to work as a group.

Work with your group to create a depiction for each of these six moments in the scenario. All the characters will be included in each depiction, so you will need to think about the spatial relationships between the characters and how that will indicate the personal relationships between them.

When you have all six depictions ready, show them in order to the other groups. Spend time discussing the ways that the different groups have presented their depictions and how this might affect the view of the scenario and the particular characters.

Ask the audience to provide a caption for each depiction, and thought balloons for each character in the depictions.

Replay the set of depictions and allow one character only to speak in each depiction. You will need to consider which character is speaking at that precise moment in each, and who that character is speaking to.

Present your depictions to the other groups with the character's line in each, then sketch these depictions in your logbook and add in the captions and thought balloons.

Spend some time discussing the issues that have been raised by these depictions. Write your ideas in your logbook.

❋ *Have you the lion's part written?*

Each of Shakespeare's players only received his own part – and his own cue lines. Only the book-holder had the entire script. Rehearsals were relatively few by today's standards and there was no director to run these. The actors understood the craft of 'playing' or 'personating', were versed in the art of rhetoric, and knew how the stage space could best be used.

These Mechanicals did not understand these aspects of the craft of acting or playing. Perhaps Shakespeare is satirising other companies in his own day, or even some of the rehearsals of his own company, with this play within the play! In showing us the inept rehearsals of these Mechanicals Shakespeare is able to demonstrate some important aspects of how to make a play.

Work in groups of six. In each group there should be one of each of the Mechanical characters.

Working as a group, read through the scene below, with the person who has been cast as each of these characters reading their lines aloud. Remember that even if the character is not speaking, he is present in the scene, listening and responding in some way to the conversation.

QUINCE	Is all our company here?
BOTTOM	You were best to call them generally, man by man, according to the scrip.
QUINCE	Here is the scroll of every man's name which is thought fit through all Athens to play in our interlude before the Duke and the Duchess on his wedding day at night.
BOTTOM	First, good Peter Quince, say what the play treats on; then read the names of the actors; and so grow to a point.
QUINCE	Marry, our play is 'The most lamentable comedy and most cruel death of Pyramus and Thisbe.'
BOTTOM	A very good piece of work, I assure you, and a merry. Now, good Peter Quince, call forth your actors by the scroll. Masters, spread yourselves.
QUINCE	Answer as I call you. Nick Bottom, the weaver?
BOTTOM	Ready. Name what part I am for, and proceed.
QUINCE	You, Nick Bottom, are set down for Pyramus.

BOTTOM	What is Pyramus? A lover or a tyrant?
QUINCE	A lover that kills himself, most gallant, for love.
BOTTOM	That will ask some tears in the true performing of it. If I do it, let the audience look to their eyes: I will move storms, I will condole, in some measure. To the rest – yet my chief humour is for a tyrant. I could play Ercles rarely, or a part to tear a cat in, to make all split:

> The raging rocks
> And shivering shocks
> Shall break the locks
>   Of prison gates,
>
> And Phibbus' car
> Shall shine from far,
> And make and mar
>   The foolish Fates.

	This was lofty. Now name the rest of the players. – This is Ercles' vein, a tyrant's vein; a lover is more condoling.
QUINCE	Francis Flute, the bellows-mender?
FLUTE	Here, Peter Quince.
QUINCE	Flute, you must take Thisbe on you.
FLUTE	What is Thisbe? A wandering knight?
QUINCE	It is the lady that Pyramus must love.
FLUTE	Nay, faith, let me not play a woman: I have a beard coming.
QUINCE	That's all one: you shall play it in a mask, and you may speak as small as you will.
BOTTOM	And I may hide my face, let me play Thisbe too. I'll speak in a monstrous little voice: 'Thisne, Thisne!' – 'Ah, Pyramus, my lover dear; thy Thisbe dear, and lady dear.'
QUINCE	No, no; you must play Pyramus; and Flute, you Thisbe.
BOTTOM	Well, proceed.
QUINCE	Robin Starveling, the tailor?
STARVELING	Here, Peter Quince.
QUINCE	Robin Starveling, you must play Thisbe's mother. Tom Snout, the tinker?
SNOUT	Here, Peter Quince.
QUINCE	You, Pyramus' father; myself, Thisbe's father; Snug, the joiner, you the lion's part; and I hope here is a play fitted.

SNUG	Have you the lion's part written? I pray you, if it be, give it me; for I am slow of study.
QUINCE	You may do it extempore; for it is nothing but roaring.
BOTTOM	Let me play the lion too. I will roar that I will do any man's heart good to hear me. I will roar that I will make the Duke say 'Let him roar again, let him roar again!'
QUINCE	And you should do it too terribly, you would fright the Duchess and the ladies that they would shriek; and that were enough to hang us all.
ALL	That would hang us, every mother's son.
BOTTOM	I grant you, friends, if you should fright the ladies out of their wits they would have no more discretion but to hang us; but I will aggravate my voice so that I will roar you as gently as any sucking dove. I will roar you and 'twere any nightingale.
QUINCE	You can play no part but Pyramus; for Pyramus is a sweet-faced man, a proper man as one shall see in a summer's day, a most lovely, gentlemanlike man: therefore you must needs play Pyramus.
BOTTOM	Well, I will undertake it. What beard were I best to play it in?
QUINCE	Why, what you will.
BOTTOM	I will discharge it in either your straw-colour beard, your orange-tawny beard, your purple-in-grain beard, or your French-crown-colour beard, your perfect yellow.
QUINCE	Some of your French crowns have no hair at all, and then you will play bare-faced. But, masters, here are your parts, and I am to entreat you, request you, and desire you to con them by tomorrow night, and meet me in the palace wood, a mile without the town, by moonlight; there will we rehearse, for if we meet in the city we shall be dogged with company, and our devices known. In the meantime I will draw a bill of properties, such as our play wants. I pray you, fail me not.
BOTTOM	We will meet, and there we may rehearse most obscenely and courageously. Take pains, be perfect: adieu!
QUINCE	At the Duke's oak we meet.
BOTTOM	Enough; hold, or cut bowstrings.

When you have had a first reading of the scene, spend some time talking about what is happening in this scene. Have another reading concentrating on the voices of the characters. Experiment with the way that Bottom's voice could change as he speaks the verses in the scene.

Talk about the characters and their personality characteristics. Write your impressions of the characters in your logbook.

※ *You may do it*

As you have seen, Bottom wants to speak everyone's part. Work with a partner or in a small group. Experiment with the voices that Bottom would need to use if he were to take the following parts:

- How would Bottom speak these lines if he were trying to take the part of Thisbe, the girl lover?

    Ah, Pyramus, my lover dear; thy Thisbe dear, and lady dear.

- How would Bottom speak these lines if he were trying to take the part of Pyramus, the male lover?

    The raging rocks
    And shivering shocks
    Shall break the locks
        Of prison gates,
    And Phibbus' car
    Shall shine from far,
    And make and mar
        The foolish fates.

- How would Bottom speak this line if he were trying to take the part of Lion?

    Roar.

- How would Bottom speak this line if he were trying to take the part of Lion, but roaring like a Nightingale?

    Roar.

Talk about the different voices and their effects.
Write your impressions of the character of Bottom in your logbook.

※ *You may do it extempore*

The working conditions of Shakespeare's actors meant that there was opportunity, and sometimes even the necessity for improvisation. In the comedies, in particular, it was common for actors to carry out more than was indicated in their scripts, and to say more than had been written down for them. Comic business was improvised.

You are going to explore some in-role improvisations.

Work in groups of six. In each group there should be one of each of the characters. Improvise a scene between these six characters that could take place when Quince is persuading them to take part in the play for the wedding.

When you have developed your improvisation, you may wish to show it to other groups.

Spend some time discussing the improvised scenes.

Each of the characters was cast by Quince as a character in a play about Pyramus and Thisbe. The scenario of this play is really a version of the story of *Romeo and Juliet*. Notice that Quince called the play: *The most lamentable comedy, and most cruel death of Pyramus and Thisbe.*

Do some research to find out about the story of Romeo and Juliet. Record this information in your logbook.

Now work in the same group as the previous scene. Each of you should adopt your Mechanical's role and then 'play' the part of the character in the Pyramus and Thisbe play.

Remember that Quince cast the Mechanicals as these characters:

BOTTOM	plays *Pyramus*
FLUTE	plays *Thisbe*
STARVELING	plays *Thisbe's mother*
SNOUT	plays *Pyramus' father*
QUINCE	plays *Thisbe's father*
SNUG	plays *Lion*

Improvise some short scenes for a play about Pyramus and Thisbe which involves these characters. Remember that this play is a comedy, but it also ends with a 'cruel death'. Remember also that Bottom spoke in verse in the scene that you improvised. You may wish to consider whether this could be incorporated in the scenes that you are developing.

When you are satisfied with your scenes, show them to others in the class. Spend some time talking about the 'plays' that you have improvised.

Record your improvisation in your logbook.

※ *This will put them out of fear*

These characters are amusing because they are so amateurish in their approach to putting on a play. The characters spend some time talking about such things as the stage space, the acting style, costumes, props and the possible effects on the audience.

One of the problems that they encounter is the difficulty of putting on a play which requires a violent death and the presence of a lion on the stage. Bottom points out:

> There are things in this comedy of Pyramus and Thisbe that will never please. First, Pyramus must draw a sword to kill himself, which the ladies cannot abide.

> ...to bring in (God shield us!) a lion among ladies is a most dreadful thing; for there is not a more fearful wildfowl than your lion living...

Work in groups of six. Each group should have one of each of the Mechanicals in it. Take on the role of the Mechanical you have worked on, and in that role discuss the problems which Bottom has raised. Try to work out how to solve these problems so that the play will not upset the ladies in the audience.

Share your solutions, out of role, with other groups. Spend some time discussing these solutions. Record your ideas in your logbook.

✳ *Prologue*

In Shakespeare's play, Bottom's solution to the problem is to write a prologue to the play. A prologue is spoken by a character, directly to the audience, before the play begins. It is usually in verse, and often tells the story or scenario of the play so that the audience knows what is going to happen, particularly if the ending is going to be tragic.

Research some of the plays written by Shakespeare that have prologues. *Romeo and Juliet* is one which does. What is the effect of the prologue for the audience?

Some plays also have an epilogue. This is spoken at the end of the play. You may also wish to research plays where Shakespeare has used epilogues. The plays *A Midsummer Night's Dream* and *Twelfth Night* both have epilogues. Why do you think Shakespeare used epilogues?

Work in your group of six. Quince has agreed to the writing of the prologue. Take on the roles of the Mechanicals again and work as a group to write the prologue for the play that you have been developing. Remember that you are to write in verse. Try to write in lines that have eight syllables. You may wish to have each line rhyme or each alternate line rhyme. Remember that you are writing this prologue so that the ladies in the audience will not be frightened by the lion or the 'cruel death' of Pyramus.

When you have completed your prologue, decide which character will speak it, and have a rehearsal before you present it to the other groups. When you present it, ask some of the members of the audience to imagine that they are the 'ladies' for whom the prologue has been written. Ask them to respond to the prologue.

Spend some time discussing whether a prologue such as this would work in the theatre today. Write your ideas in your logbook.

❀ *He comes to disfigure*

The Mechanicals have some other practical problems with their play. Quince points out these problems:

> ...to bring the moonlight into a chamber; for, you know, Pyramus and Thisbe meet by moonlight

and,

> ...we must have a wall in the great chamber; for Pyramus and Thisbe, says the story, did talk through the chink of a wall.

The great chamber is the room in the palace where the Mechanicals are to perform their play. Quince is pointing out the problem that, in a play, it is not possible realistically to present objects and places and even actions on the stage.

Work in a group. Talk about why the wall and the moonlight might be so significant to the story.

Discuss how you could solve this problem in Shakespeare's day with the technology then available, and how you might be able to solve the problem today with contemporary technology.

Share your solutions with others in the class.

The solution that the Mechanicals come to is that actors or players must represent the wall and the moonlight:

> ...one must come in with a bush of thorns and a lantern, and say he comes to disfigure, or to present the person of Moonshine.

> Some man or other must present Wall; and let him have some plaster, or some loam, or some rough-cast about him to signify Wall; or let him hold his fingers thus, and through that cranny shall Pyramus and Thisbe whisper.

Do some research to find out why Moonshine is represented by a bush of thorns and a lantern. Later in the play, Moonshine is also given a 'dog'. Discuss why this might occur.

Work in small groups to design costumes for the characters of Wall and Moonshine. Present your sketches to the others in the group. Decide on which costumes work best to represent the wall and moonshine in the play.

Record your decisions in your logbook with the reasons for them.

✖ *What sayest thou, bully Bottom?*

Work in your group of six. You should each take on the role of the Mechanical character again. Having decided that you will solve the problem of the prologue and of representing the wall and the moonshine using actors, you now do not have enough players for each of the original parts. Three of the characters will have to give up their parts to play Prologue, Wall and Moonshine.

Improvise a scene where the Mechanicals deal with this new problem and work out a way of solving it.

Out of role, discuss how the problem has been solved. Consider how this will change the nature of the play that you are to present.

Record your discoveries in your logbook.

✖ *Are we all met?*

You may now wish to read the scene in which the Mechanicals meet to discuss the problems of putting on the play.

BOTTOM	Are we all met?
QUINCE	Pat, pat; and here's a marvellous convenient place for our rehearsal. This green plot shall be our stage, this hawthorn brake our tiring-house, and we will do it in action as we will do it before the Duke.
BOTTOM	Peter Quince!
QUINCE	What sayest thou, bully Bottom?
BOTTOM	There are things in this comedy of Pyramus and Thisbe that will never please. First, Pyramus must draw a sword to kill himself, which the ladies cannot abide. How answer you that?
SNOUT	By'r lakin, a parlous fear!
STARVELING	I believe we must leave the killing out, when all is done.
BOTTOM	Not a whit; I have a device to make all well. Write me a prologue, and let the prologue seem to say we will do no harm with our swords, and that Pyramus is not killed indeed; and for the more better assurance, tell them that I, Pyramus, am not Pyramus, but Bottom the weaver: this will put them out of fear.
QUINCE	Well, we will have such a prologue; and it shall be written in eight and six.

BOTTOM	No, make it two more: let it be written in eight and eight.
SNOUT	Will not the ladies be afeared of the lion?
STARVELING	I fear it, I promise you.
BOTTOM	Masters, you ought to consider with yourself, to bring in (God shield us!) a lion among ladies is a most dreadful thing; for there is not a more fearful wildfowl than your lion living; and we ought to look to't.
SNOUT	Therefore another prologue must tell he is not a lion.
BOTTOM	Nay, you must name his name, and half his face must be seen through the lion's neck, and he himself must speak through, saying thus, or to the same defect, 'Ladies', or 'Fair ladies, I would wish you', or 'I would request you', or 'I would entreat you, not to fear, not to tremble: my life for yours. If you think I come hither as a lion, it were pity on my life. No, I am no such thing; I am a man, as other men are' – and there indeed let him name his name, and tell them plainly he is Snug the joiner.
QUINCE	Well, it shall be so. But there is two hard things: that is, to bring the moonlight into a chamber; for, you know, Pyramus and Thisbe meet by moonlight.
SNOUT	Doth the moon shine that night we play our play?
BOTTOM	A calendar, a calendar! Look in the almanac – find out moonshine, find out moonshine!
QUINCE	Yes, it doth shine that night.
BOTTOM	Why, then you may leave a casement of the great chamber window, where we play, open, and the moon may shine in at the casement.
QUINCE	Ay; or else one must come in with a bush of thorns and a lantern, and say he comes to disfigure, or to present the person of Moonshine. Then there is another thing: we must have a wall in the great chamber; for Pyramus and Thisbe, says the story, did talk through the chink of a wall.
SNUG	You can never bring in a wall. What say you, Bottom?
BOTTOM	Some man or other must present Wall; and let him have some plaster, or some loam, or some rough-cast about him to signify Wall; or let him hold his fingers thus, and through that cranny shall Pyramus and Thisbe whisper.

QUINCE   If that may be, then all is well. Come, sit down every mother's son, and rehearse your parts. Pyramus, you begin. When you have spoken your speech, enter into that brake, and so everyone according to his cue.

Record your explorations in your logbook.

✶ A tedious brief scene

In Shakespeare's play the Mechanicals manage to rehearse and perform a play at the wedding which has a Prologue and players to represent Wall and Moonshine. Ultimately the actors or players adjust their parts.
The final casting is:

QUINCE   plays *Prologue*

SNOUT   plays *Wall*

BOTTOM   plays *Pyramus*

FLUTE   plays *Thisbe*

SNUG   plays *Lion*

STARVELING   plays *Moonshine*

Work in six groups. Each group should consist of all the people playing one of the Mechanicals. In role, discuss the part that you have been allocated. Talk about the role of this character in the 'lamentable comedy'. Discuss the costume that the character could use to help portray the personality to the audience.
Experiment with voice and movement for the character. Remember that you are playing a role within a role, i.e. Bottom playing Pyramus.
Improvise scenes that might be part of this play. Share some of your improvisations with other groups. Talk about the types of plays that you have been constructing.
Record your improvisations in your logbook.

✶ Quince's Prologue

The prologue to a play often told the story or scenario of the play, so that the audience knew what would happen. Quince's Prologue tells the story of the play, although it is not well written. Perhaps Shakespeare was sending up other writers of his time who did not produce such neat prologues as he was able to do.

Work in groups. Read through the Prologue printed below. As you read through these lines, notice the poetic form. The lines each have ten syllables in them. There is a regular pattern of stressed and unstressed syllables. This was the verse form that Shakespeare used throughout his plays. It is called 'blank verse' or 'unrhymed iambic pentameter'.

You may wish to consult chapter 1 for further information about Shakespeare's blank verse.

When you read these lines, try to keep the rhythmic pattern moving. It is a good idea to read to the end of the line and to give the last iambic foot in the line the primary stress.

Gentles, perchance you wonder at this *show*.

Quince's verse, however, is not very well written. He has muddled much of the punctuation and this interrupts the meaning and makes it difficult to speak. It also provides a great deal of the humour as he gets it wrong.

Talk about the scenario that the Prologue presents. Discuss how many scenes you will need to construct this play. Improvise these scenes.

Show your versions of the play to others in the class. Discuss the interpretations of the scenario.

QUINCE (*as Prologue*)

> If we offend, it is with our good will.
> That you should think, we come not to offend,
> But with good will. To show our simple skill,
>   That is the true beginning of our end.
> Consider then, we come but in despite.
>   We do not come as minding to content you,
> Our true intent is. All for your delight,
>   We are not here. That you should here repent you,
> The actors are at hand; and by their show
> You shall know all that you are like to know.
> Gentles, perchance you wonder at this show,
> But wonder on, till truth make all things plain.
> This man is Pyramus, if you would know;
>   This beauteous lady Thisbe is, certain.
> This man with lime and rough-cast doth present
>   Wall, that vile wall which did these lovers sunder;
> And through Wall's chink, poor souls, they are content
>   To whisper – at the which let no man wonder.
> This man with lanthorn, dog, and bush of thorn,
>   Presenteth Moonshine; for, if you will know,
> By moonshine did these lovers think no scorn
>   To meet at Ninus' tomb, there, there to woo.
> This grisly beast, which Lion hight by name,
>   The trusty Thisbe, coming first by night,

Did scare away, or rather did affright;
And as she fled, her mantle she did fall,
    Which Lion vile with bloody mouth did stain.
Anon comes Pyramus, sweet youth and tall,
    And finds his trusty Thisbe's mantle slain;
Whereat with blade, with bloody, blameful blade,
    He bravely broached his boiling bloody breast;
And Thisbe, tarrying in mulberry shade,
    His dagger drew, and died. For all the rest,
Let Lion, Moonshine, Wall and lovers twain
At large discourse, while here they do remain.

Record your impressions in your logbook.

✳ *You wonder at this show*

As Quince speaks the Prologue the other players come on to the stage. Notice that as Quince relates the scenario of the play, he is also introducing each of the characters. In a way, he is actually directing the play from this moment. Quince does not speak again in the play. You might like to consider whether he continues to 'direct' the play from the sidelines as the actors proceed.

Work in groups of six. Work out how this Prologue scene could be presented to the audience. You will need to think about each of the characters and how they would present themselves to the audience. Remember that these are not professional actors playing the part and the characters or personalities of the men would show through their performance of the roles in the play. You may need to remind yourselves of the key personality features of each actor.

When you have blocked each moment in the Prologue, rehearse it and present it to others in the class.

Talk about how the audience might respond to this presentation. Record your ideas in your logbook.

✳ *In this same interlude*

Each player in Shakespeare's day received only his own lines and cue lines. Talk about how this might affect the way that the player understood what was happening in the play.

Below you will find the parts for three of the characters in the play. The parts contain only the lines which the character speaks and the cue lines, printed in italics, which indicate when he is to speak. Within the lines there are also indications as to actions and movements.

Notice that the lines which Snout/Wall speaks are also in iambic pentameter, but that they use rhyming couplets. Read these lines, stressing the rhyming words at the end of each line. Consider how the sounds of these rhyming words affect the meaning and mood.

Explore what shape the 'crannied hole or chink' might be. Think about how the actor might have made this hole. Notice that Snout/Wall's last line indicates his exit.

Notice that the lines of Snug/Lion are also in iambic pentameter and that there is also some rhyme used, although this differs from the rhyming couplets of Snout/Wall's lines. Think about how Snug/Lion actually roars. Remember Snug's character! Talk about the effect that it would have on an audience if the roar of the lion were soft and gentle as opposed to loud and fearsome.

Look closely at the lines which Starveling/Moonshine speaks. He begins his lines and then pauses. He starts again and gets a little further. Notice that the third part is in prose. Discuss what this tells us about the character of Starveling.

Work in three groups. Each group should select one of the sets of lines. Read through the lines and work out what the character is doing at each stage of the speech. You will also need to think about who else might be on the stage at this point in time. When you are confident that you understand what is happening in the speech, rehearse it with appropriate voice and actions. Show the rehearsed parts to the rest of the class. Talk about how you managed to work out what was happening in the speeches and in the scene.

SNOUT (as Wall)   *At large discourse, while here they do remain.*
                   In this same interlude it doth befall
                   That I, one Snout by name, present a wall;
                   And such a wall, as I would have you think
                   That had in it a crannied hole or chink,
                   Through which the lovers, Pyramus and Thisbe,
                   Did whisper often, very secretly.
                   This loam, this rough-cast, and this stone doth show
                   That I am that same wall; the truth is so.
                   And this the cranny is, right and sinister,
                   Through which the fearful lovers are to whisper.
                   Tide life, tide death, I come without delay.
                   Thus have I, Wall, my part dischargèd so;
                   And being done, thus Wall away doth go.

SNUG (as Lion)   *...thus Wall away doth go.*
                   You ladies, you whose gentle hearts do fear
                   The smallest monstrous mouse that creeps on floor,
                   May now perchance both quake and tremble here,
                   When lion rough in wildest rage doth roar.

> Then know that I one Snug the joiner am
> A lion fell, nor else no lion's dam:
> For if I should as lion come in strife
> Into this place, 'twere pity on my life.
> *...Where is my love?*
> Roar!

STARVELING (*as Moonshine*)
> *...'twere pity on my life.*
> This lanthorn doth the hornèd moon present –
> This lanthorn doth the hornèd moon present;
> Myself the man i'th'moon do seem to be –
> All that I have to say is to tell you that the lanthorn is the
> moon, I the man i'th'moon, this thorn bush my thorn
> bush, and this dog my dog.

Record your explorations and discoveries in your logbook.

✖ *Asleep, my love?*

The key characters in this play are, of course, the two lovers. These two characters make their entrances and exits and interact not only with each other, but also with the other characters.

Below you will find the lines and cue lines for the two lovers. Work in small groups. Select one of the characters and explore what is happening in each of the speeches. Look closely at the cue lines to see who is speaking before and after each speech. Rehearse the lines, imagining the other characters on the stage. Remember that Bottom plays Pyramus and Flute plays Thisbe.

BOTTOM (*as Pyramus*)
> *Through which the fearful lovers are to whisper.*
> O grim-looked night, O night with hue so black,
>   O night which ever art when day is not!
> O night, O night, alack, alack, alack,
>   I fear my Thisbe's promise is forgot!
> And thou, O wall, O sweet, O lovely wall,
>   That stand'st between her father's ground and mine,
> Thou wall, O wall, O sweet and lovely wall,
>   Show me thy chink, to blink through with mine eyne.
> Thanks, courteous wall; Jove shield thee well for this!
>   But what see I? No Thisbe do I see.
> O wicked wall, through whom I see no bliss,
>   Cursed be thy stones for thus deceiving me!
> *Thy stones with lime and hair knit up in thee.*

I see a voice: now will I to the chink,
   To spy and I can hear my Thisbe's face.
Thisbe!
My love! Thou art my love, I think?
Think what thou wilt, I am thy lover's grace,
And like Limander am I trusty still.
...till the Fates me kill.
Not Shafalus to Procrus was so true.
...I to you.
O, kiss me through the hole of this vile wall!
...not your lips at all.
Wilt thou at Ninny's tomb meet me straightway?
Roar.
Sweet moon, I thank thee for thy sunny beams;
   I thank thee, moon, for shining now so bright;
For by thy gracious, golden, glittering gleams
   I trust to take of truest Thisbe sight.
      But stay – O spite!
      But mark, poor Knight,
What dreadful dole is here?
      Eyes, do you see?
      How can it be?
O dainty duck, O dear!
      Thy mantle good –
      What, stained with blood?
Approach, ye Furies fell!
      O Fates, come, come,
      Cut thread and thrum,
   Quail, crush, conclude, and quell.
O wherefore, Nature, didst thou lions frame,
   Since lion vile hath here deflowered my dear?
Which is – no, no – which was the fairest dame
   That lived, that loved, that liked, that looked with
cheer.
         Come tears, confound!
         Out sword, and wound
   The pap of Pyramus,
      Ay, that left pap,
      Where heart doth hop:
Thus die I, thus, thus, thus!
      Now am I dead,
      Now am I fled;
   My soul is in the sky.
      Tongue, lose thy light;
      Moon, take thy flight;
   Now die, die, die, die, die.

FLUTE (*as Thisbe*)

Cursed be thy stones for thus deceiving me!
O wall, full often hast thou heard my moans,
  For parting my fair Pyramus and me.
My cherry lips have often kissed thy stones,
  Thy stones with lime and hair knit up in thee.
Thisbe!
My love! Thou art my love, I think?
...am I trusty still.
And like Helen, till the Fates me kill.
...was so true.
As Shafalus to Procrus, I to you.
...the hole of this vile wall!
I kiss the wall's hole, not your lips at all.
...meet me straightway?
Tide life, tide death, I come without delay.
...this thorn bush my thorn bush, and this dog my dog.
This is old Ninny's tomb. Where is my love?
Roar.
Now die, die, die, die, die.
  Asleep, my love?
  What, dead, my dove?
 O Pyramus, arise.
  Speak, speak! Quite dumb?
  Dead, dead! A tomb
Must cover thy sweet eyes.
  These lily lips,
  This cherry nose,
These yellow cowslip cheeks
  Are gone, are gone.
    Lovers, make moan;
  His eyes were green as leeks.
   O sisters three,
   Come, come to me
 With hands as pale as milk;
 Lay them in gore,
 Since you have shore
With shears his thread of silk.
  Tongue, not a word!
  Come, trusty sword,
Come blade, my breast imbrue!
  And farewell, friends.
  Thus Thisbe ends –
Adieu, adieu, adieu!

Record your impressions in your logbook.

✳ *Tide life, tide death*

Work in groups of six. The full script of *Pyramus and Thisbe* is printed
below. It is divided into rehearsal units. In your group, cast the roles of the
play. Remember that these are roles within roles, e.g. Bottom plays Pyramus.
Rehearse each unit of the play. Remember that this is a 'lamentable comedy'.
You will need to explore appropriate actions and interactions for the
characters. When you are satisfied with your rehearsals, present the whole
play to other groups in the class, or to an outside audience. Notice how the
audience reacts to your play. Hold an actors' forum or talk informally with
audience members afterwards to get some feedback on your performances.

Unit 1

You have already explored this Prologue. Explore how the characters might
respond to the types of introductions which Quince makes for each of them.
Think about how you could set the mood for the 'lamentable comedy'
through comic business in this Prologue.

Explore what Quince does as he introduces the cast and the story. Notice
that he is talking directly to the audience. Talk about where he is at the end
of the Prologue. Does he remain on stage? Does he stand in the wings, side-
coaching the action? Does he go into the audience?

Explore what the other characters do at the end of the Prologue. Do they
remain on stage?

QUINCE (*as Prologue*)
>   If we offend, it is with our good will.
>   That you should think, we come not to offend,
>   But with good will. To show our simple skill,
>   That is the true beginning of our end.
>   Consider then, we come but in despite.
>   We do not come as minding to content you,
>   Our true intent is. All for your delight,
>   We are not here. That you should here repent you,
>   The actors are at hand; and by their show
>   You shall know all that you are like to know.
>   Gentles, perchance you wonder at this show,
>   But wonder on, till truth make all things plain.
>   This man is Pyramus, if you would know;
>   This beauteous lady Thisbe is, certain.
>   This man with lime and rough-cast doth present
>   Wall, that vile wall which did these lovers sunder;
>   And through Wall's chink, poor souls, they are content
>   To whisper – at the which let no man wonder.
>   This man with lanthorn, dog, and bush of thorn,

Presenteth Moonshine; for, if you will know,
By moonshine did these lovers think no scorn
    To meet at Ninus' tomb, there, there to woo.
This grisly beast, which Lion hight by name,
The trusty Thisbe, coming first by night,
Did scare away, or rather did affright;
And as she fled, her mantle she did fall,
    Which Lion vile with bloody mouth did stain.
Anon comes Pyramus, sweet youth and tall,
    And finds his trusty Thisbe's mantle slain;
Whereat with blade, with bloody, blameful blade,
    He bravely broached his boiling bloody breast;
And Thisbe, tarrying in mulberry shade,
    His dagger drew, and died. For all the rest,
Let Lion, Moonshine, Wall and lovers twain
At large discourse, while here they do remain.

Unit 2

Explore where Snout/Wall would be on the stage. Is Wall facing the audience, or is he side-on to the audience? What difference will it make to the audience if Wall stands still or moves as Snout speaks the lines? Experiment with the shape of the 'chink'. What difference does it make to the idea of 'kissing the wall's hole' if the shape is round, or a slit?

SNOUT (*as Wall*)

In this same interlude it doth befall
That I, one Snout by name, present a wall;
And such a wall, as I would have you think
That had in it a crannied hole or chink,
Through which the lovers, Pyramus and Thisbe,
Did whisper often, very secretly.
This loam, this rough-cast, and this stone doth show
That I am that same wall; the truth is so.
And this the cranny is, right and sinister,
Through which the fearful lovers are to whisper.

Unit 3

Bottom's speech has many repetitions, particularly the word 'O'. Explore ways that these could be said. What gestures might be appropriate to these lines? What is Wall doing while Bottom is speaking? Is there any comic business for Wall in this unit? How does Wall respond to Bottom's last lines?

BOTTOM (*as Pyramus*)

> O grim-looked night, O night with hue so black,
>> O night, which ever art when day is not!
> O night, O night, alack, alack, alack,
>> I fear my Thisbe's promise is forgot!
> And thou, O wall, O sweet, O lovely wall,
>> That stand'st between her father's ground and mine,
> Thou wall, O wall, O sweet and lovely wall,
>> Show me thy chink, to blink through with mine eyne.
> Thanks, courteous wall; Jove shield thee well for this!
>> But what see I? No Thisbe do I see.
> O wicked wall, through whom I see no bliss,
>> Cursed be thy stones for thus deceiving me!

Unit 4

Where does Thisbe enter from? What does Wall do when she speaks? What is Bottom doing during this speech? Where is Quince during this speech?

FLUTE (*as Thisbe*)

> O wall, full often hast thou heard my moans,
>> For parting my fair Pyramus and me.
> My cherry lips have often kissed thy stones,
>> Thy stones with lime and hair knit up in thee.

Unit 5

Bottom/Pyramus and Flute/Thisbe now interact with Wall between them. Notice that they compare themselves to famous lovers. You may wish to replace the allusions to the legendary lovers Hero and Leander with the names of famous contemporary lovers to see what the effect might be.

This is a love scene about passionate young love. Remember that these are two boy actors, playing two male parts, taking on the role of the lovers. Look at the interactions between the lovers. Experiment with ways of making this passionate. Is this moment meant to be played 'straight', or is there a satiric aspect to it?

Explore how Wall reacts to the lovers. Where is Quince in this scene?

BOTTOM (*as Pyramus*)

> Thisbe!

FLUTE (*as Thisbe*)

> My love! Thou art my love, I think?

BOTTOM (*as Pyramus*)

> Think what thou wilt, I am thy lover's grace,
> And like Limander am I trusty still.

FLUTE (*as Thisbe*)
>And I like Helen, till the Fates me kill.

BOTTOM (*as Pyramus*)
>Not Shafalus to Procrus was so true.

FLUTE (*as Thisbe*)
>As Shafalus to Procrus, I to you.

BOTTOM (*as Pyramus*)
>O, kiss me through the hole of this vile wall!

FLUTE (*as Thisbe*)
>I kiss the wall's hole, not your lips at all.

BOTTOM (*as Pyramus*)
>Wilt thou at Ninny's tomb meet me straightway?

FLUTE (*as Thisbe*)
>Tide life, tide death, I come without delay.

SNOUT (*as Wall*)
>Thus have I, Wall, my part dischargèd so;
>And being done, thus Wall away doth go.

Unit 6

Think about Snug's character. How would a man with his personality play the part of Lion. Think about his voice and movements. Remember he is talking to the audience. Where is he on the stage? Where is Quince? Where is Lion at the end of his speech? Does he go off? Does he take up a position on the stage? Does he interact with Moonshine?

SNUG (*as Lion*)
>You ladies, you whose gentle hearts do fear
>>The smallest monstrous mouse that creeps on floor,
>May now, perchance, both quake and tremble here,
>>When Lion rough in wildest rage doth roar.
>Then know that I as Snug the joiner am
>A lion fell, nor else no lion's dam;
>For if I should as lion come in strife
>Into this place, 'twere pity on my life.

Unit 7

Talk about the personality of Starveling. How does a man with his personality play this part in the play? What is Quince doing during this speech? How does Starveling say these lines? What does he do between each set of lines? What does he do at the end of the lines?

STARVELING (*as Moonshine*)

> This lanthorn doth the hornèd moon present –
> This lanthorn doth the hornèd moon present;
>> Myself the man i'th'moon do seem to be –
> All that I have to say is to tell you that the lanthorn is
> the moon, I the man i'th'moon, this thorn bush my
> thorn bush, and this dog my dog.

Unit 8

The entrance of Flute/Thisbe is critical to the humour. There are few words spoken here, but there is some vital activity. Explore how she enters and from where? Where is her mantle? Where is Moonshine? Does she react to Moonshine? Where is Snug/Lion? Does he react to her? What happens to the mantle? How does it get stained with blood? Do they both run away? In which directions could they run? What does Moonshine do? Where is Quince?

FLUTE (*as Thisbe*)

> This is old Ninny's tomb. Where is my love?

SNUG (*as Lion*)

> Roar.

Unit 9

Where does Bottom/Pyramus enter from? How does he interact with Moonshine? Where is Thisbe's 'mantle'? What does Pyramus do with the mantle after he finds the blood? How does he create his death scene? Where is the sword when he enters? When does Moonshine leave the stage? How does he leave? Where is Bottom/Pyramus at the end of the speech?

BOTTOM (*as Pyramus*)

> Sweet moon, I thank thee for thy sunny beams;
> I thank thee, moon, for shining now so bright;
> For by thy gracious, golden, glittering gleams
>> I trust to take of truest Thisbe sight.
>>> But stay – O spite!
>>> But mark, poor Knight,
>> What dreadful dole is here?
>>> Eyes, do you see?
>>> How can it be?
>> O dainty duck, O dear!
>>> Thy mantle good –
>>> What, stained with blood?
> Approach, ye Furies fell!

O Fates, come, come,
Cut thread and thrum,
Quail, crush, conclude, and quell.
O wherefore, Nature, didst thou lions frame,
Since lion vile hath here deflowered my dear?
Which is – no, no – which was the fairest dame
That lived, that loved, that liked, that looked with
cheer.
Come tears, confound!
Out sword, and wound
The pap of Pyramus,
Ay, that left pap,
Where heart doth hop:
Thus die I, thus, thus, thus!
Now am I dead,
Now am I fled;
My soul is in the sky.
Tongue, lose thy light;
Moon, take thy flight;
Now die, die, die, die, die.

Unit 10

At what point and from where does Thisbe enter? How does she react to
Bottom/Pyramus? Is Bottom/Pyramus motionless during this speech? How
does she get hold of the sword? How does she kill herself?

FLUTE *(as Thisbe)*

Asleep, my love?
What, dead, my dove?
O Pyramus, arise.
Speak, speak! Quite dumb?
Dead, dead! A tomb
Must cover thy sweet eyes.
These lily lips,
This cherry nose,
These yellow cowslip cheeks
Are gone, are gone.
Lovers, make moan;
His eyes were green as leeks.
O sisters three,
Come, come to me
With hands as pale as milk;
Lay them in gore,
Since you have shore

With shears his thread of silk.
Tongue, not a word!
Come, trusty sword,
Come blade, my breast imbrue!
And farewell, friends.
Thus Thisbe ends –
Adieu, adieu, adieu!

✳ Will it please you to see the epilogue?

This play began with a prologue. Does it need an epilogue? An epilogue would round off the action and perhaps point out the moral of the story.

Work in small groups and discuss what kind of epilogue the play could have. Think about who could speak the epilogue. Look at the kind of verse that was used for the prologue. Think about how the prologue introduced the characters. Can your epilogue also allow all the characters to be back on the stage?

Write an epilogue using lines with iambic pentameter. Rehearse your epilogue and add it to the play.

✳ A most lamentable comedy

Look back over the work that you have done. Reread your logbook entries. As a group, make a decision about the scenes that you could put together to make a playbuilt play. You may decide to select from the scenes with the Mechanicals in the process of the development of their play. Alternatively, you may wish to use only the play within the play.

The scenes you have explored include:

- character monologues
- casting scenario
- first version of the play
- prologue
- wall and moonlight problem
- rehearsal scene
- play within the play
- epilogue.

Casting

You may wish to retain the roles which you have worked with throughout these workshop activities, or you may wish to recast the play.

Rehearsing

Once you have decided on the scenes, you will need to revisit these, rehearsing each moment or unit, tightening up any timing or movement and working on the speech.

Linking the scenes

When all the individual scenes are well rehearsed, have a complete run-through of this playbuilt play. Shakespeare did not have breaks in between scenes and one scene flowed into the next without a pause. You should attempt to do the same. You may need to consider the best ways to make this happen. Consider whether linking devices such as music are necessary between the scenes.

Performing

When you have thoroughly rehearsed the play, present it to an audience and encourage the audience to give you feedback on their responses to the play.

You may wish to develop a printed program that provides your audience with information that you have explored throughout the playbuilding process.

Write your own responses to the play and the playbuilding process that you have gone through in your logbook. Keep a copy of the final script that you used for your performance.

When you have presented your version of the story, you may wish to explore the rest of Shakespeare's play, *A Midsummer Night's Dream*.

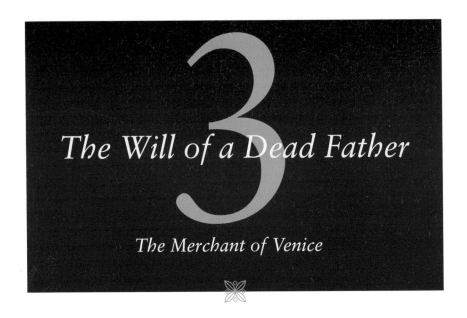

The Will of a Dead Father

The Merchant of Venice

In this unit of work you are going to explore a love story from one of Shakespeare's plays – *The Merchant of Venice*. In this love story the girl is constrained by her father's will so that she is unable to select her own marriage partner. This form of arranged marriage probably does not commonly occur today, as women are no longer seen as property owned by men. But there are other forms of arranged marriages that do occur today.

✳ *Preliminary discussion*

Work with a small group. Talk about arranged marriages both in an historical context and in contemporary society. What arranged marriages do you know about? How successful might arranged marriages be in modern societies? Which societies do you know about which still arrange the marriages of their young people? Do some research about the traditions of arranged marriages and the reasons for them.

Talk about how arranged marriages might affect the partners and their attitudes towards each other. How much say should parents have in the choice of marriage partners for their sons and daughters?

Write your ideas in your logbook.

❈ *The will of a dead father*

The will of a dead person is considered a legally binding document. It usually dictates to those still living what is to be done with the property of the deceased.

Read the following excerpt from a will. Work with a partner to discuss how you would feel if you were the daughter in this case.

> I bequeath to my only daughter, Portia, all my property including the house and its contents, and all my money and wealth, upon condition that she never may marry.

Improvise a scene in which one of you plays the daughter and the other plays a friend. The improvisation should show how the daughter and friend feel about the terms of this father's will.

You might like to try out several possible scenarios. Spend some time talking about each one.

Present one of your improvisations to the class. What issues have been raised by these improvisations? Write your thoughts in your logbook.

You may wish to look at the play, *The Merchant of Venice*, Act 1 Scene 2, where Nerissa and Portia discuss a similar situation.

Write your responses to the scene in your logbook.

❈ *I may not choose*

The following line comes from *The Merchant of Venice*:

> I may neither choose who I would, nor refuse who I dislike.

It is spoken by Portia, the daughter whose father's will prevents her from choosing her own marriage partner.

Work with a partner. Imagine that you are Portia. Explore how she might say this line.

Consider whether there is bitterness or anger or frustration or some other emotion in the line. Try out a number of different ways that Portia might speak the line. You may wish to refer to the section on antithesis in chapter 1. Experiment with facial expressions, gestures, body language and movement.

How might Portia speak the line to a friend? How would she speak it to her father? How would she speak it to one of the suitors who was seeking her hand in marriage?

Present your versions of the line to the rest of the class. Ask your audience to discuss the feelings expressed through the voice, gesture and movement.

Write your ideas in your logbook.

✻ *The will of a living daughter*

Work with your partner. One of you should play the part of the girl and the other play the part of the father. Imagine that you have just been given the news that your father has placed these conditions upon your marriage partner in his will. Consider why a father might do this. How might his daughter react to the action?

Improvise a scene between the father and daughter in which you explore the situation and the father's and daughter's feelings.

Show your scene to other groups in the class. Discuss the issues raised in all the scenes presented.

Write an outline of the scenario that you have improvised in your journal. You may wish to include some of the lines that were actually spoken in the presentation of the scenario to the class.

✻ *Who chooses his meaning*

Read the scenario of *The Merchant of Venice* below. As you read this scenario, ask yourself how you would feel if you were Portia.

Portia is a wealthy heiress who is rather unhappy. Her father has died and left her a vast fortune in his will but he has also laid down some conditions that will affect the rest of her life and particularly her future marriage. The terms of her father's will prevent her from choosing her own husband. Her father has decreed in his will that any man who desires to marry her must make a formal selection from one of three caskets that he has set up as a kind of test for any would-be suitor. The will is a legally binding document that makes it impossible for Portia to disobey, unless she is prepared to lose the not inconsiderable fortune.

The caskets are not identical. One casket is made of gold, one of silver and one of lead. On the outside of each casket is an inscription.

The gold casket bears the inscription:

Who chooseth me, shall gain what many men desire.

The silver casket bears the inscription:

Who chooseth me, shall get as much as he deserves.

The lead casket bears the inscription:

Who chooseth me, must give and hazard all he hath.

Within each casket is a scroll and an image. Within one casket is the image of a fool, within another is the image of a skull, and within another is the image of Portia herself.

The suitor who selects the casket that contains the image or picture of Portia is the one who may marry her. Portia does not have the right to refuse this suitor.

Any suitor who comes to woo Portia and make a selection from the caskets has to enter into a contract. This contract binds him, if he chooses the wrong casket, to leave immediately, never revealing which casket he chose and never pursuing another woman by way of marriage. If he chooses correctly, of course, he wins the hand of Portia in marriage.

Many suitors come to woo Portia and she is bored and annoyed by them. Fortunately most of them go away when they learn the conditions that they must agree to before seeing the caskets. Portia, of course, knows which is the correct casket, but she is also bound by her promise to her father not to reveal this information to any of the suitors.

But two suitors are undeterred by the conditions. They are the Prince of Morocco and the Prince of Arragon. Fortunately they make wrong choices, Morocco choosing the gold casket and Arragon choosing the silver casket, and they are required to leave.

As luck has it, a suitor whom she knows and likes, Bassanio, approaches to make the choice. Portia is thrilled and excited but also worried that if he chooses incorrectly she will lose him. She tries to delay his choosing so that she can spend time with him, and she even contemplates giving him hints as to the casket he should choose. But he is keen to make a choice, and fortunately for Portia, who has already fallen in love with him, his labour in choosing the lead casket is rewarded with the picture of Portia, and therefore her hand in marriage.

This, of course, demonstrates the wisdom of her father's will and the conditions that he imposed upon her!

Or does it? Write your ideas in your logbook.

Who chooseth me

Work with a small group. Talk about this scenario. Could it happen today? Could it happen in other countries? What do you think might have happened if another suitor had chosen the correct casket? How might Portia have felt if either Arragon or Morocco had chosen the correct casket?

What other issues does this story raise for you? Make a list of these issues. What answers does the story give to them?

Does this kind of happy-ever-after scenario only happen in stories?

Write your ideas in your logbook.

✳ *Gold, silver and base lead*

Think about the caskets and the three different metals they were made from. Talk about the qualities of these metals. What kind of metal is gold? What kind of metal is silver? What kind of metal is lead?

Do some research to find out the characteristics of these three metals. Research their qualities, what they are used for and how different cultures value these metals in ornamentation.

Try to find references to these metals in other stories or in poetry.

Present the information from your research either as a talk or as a poster.

✳ *All that glisters*

Work in small groups. Discuss the type of casket that could be made from the metals. What might each casket look like? What ideas are associated with each of the three caskets?

Write your ideas in your logbook.

✳ *What many men desire*

Work in groups of three. Reread the inscriptions that were engraved on each of the caskets. Read the words that were on the scrolls inside each of the caskets, printed below.

The gold casket bears the inscription:

Who chooseth me, shall gain what many men desire.

The scroll contains these words:

All that glisters is not gold;
Often have you heard that told.
Many a man his life hath sold
But my outside to behold.
Gilded tombs do worms infold.
Had you been as wise as bold,
Young in limbs, in judgement old,
Your answer had not been inscrolled.
Fare you well, your suit is cold.

The silver casket bears the inscription:

Who chooseth me, shall get as much as he deserves.

The scroll contains these words:

> The fire seven times tried this;
> Seven times tried that judgement is
> That did never choose amiss.
> Some there be that shadows kiss;
> Such have but a shadow's bliss.
> There be fools alive iwis,
> Silvered o'er, and so was this.
> Take what wife you will to bed,
> I will ever be your head.
> So be gone; you are sped.

The lead casket bears the inscription:

> Who chooseth me, must give and hazard all he hath.

The scroll contains these words:

> You that choose not by the view
> Chance as fair, and choose as true.
> Since this fortune falls to you,
> Be content and seek no new.
> If you be well pleased with this,
> And hold your fortune for your bliss,
> Turn you where your lady is,
> And claim her with a loving kiss.

Experiment with reading each of these aloud. Experiment with ways in which each suitor might read these words. How would Morocco and Arragon read the words on the scrolls as they realise that they have chosen the wrong caskets? How would Bassanio read the words on the scroll as he realises he has chosen correctly? Discuss what effect these words might have on each of the suitors.

Talk about the differences in the meanings of the scrolls. Look closely at the rhyme scheme in each of the scrolls. Try out ways of reading the lines so that you emphasise the rhymed words and point out the irony of the meaning. You may wish to refer to chapter 1 for further information about rhyme.

Write your ideas in your logbook.

✳ *Chance as fair*

Work in groups. You are going to work as props designers for a play. The designer's job is to communicate ideas to the audience through the visual language of the props. Different colours, lines, textures and shapes communicate different ideas to an audience.

Discuss what the caskets in the story might symbolise. Talk about the characteristics of each metal, the inscription that was attached to each and the words on the scrolls that were inside each casket. Talk about the ideas that are associated with each of the three caskets.

Your task is to design caskets in each of the three metals that would show these ideas. Write a brief statement of the meanings of the casket and sketch the design for the three caskets.

Talk about the scrolls and the images that were inside the caskets and the keys that would open each casket. Discuss what these might look like.

When you are satisfied that your sketches for the design of each casket represent the ideas associated with each of the caskets you should work out how to make the three caskets according to your design.

When you have completed the construction of the three caskets, the three scrolls, the three images and the three keys, display them for others in the class. Discuss the ideas that each design suggests to the viewers.

Record your designs and your ideas in your logbook.

✲ *Must give and hazard all he hath*

Work in the same groups using the caskets that you have constructed.

You are now going to use the caskets in a ritualised scene. You are going to construct a ritual ceremony set on the father's deathbed.

Ritual involves a ceremony where actions, words and objects may take on symbolic significance. Think about some of the rituals that you encounter in daily life, such as those used in churches, in schools or in public ceremonies. Talk about the actions, words and objects that are part of the rituals or ceremonies that you are familiar with.

The ritualised ceremony that you are going to construct will involve the announcement of the father's will that binds the daughter into the lottery of the caskets. The ceremony will also involve the handing over of the caskets and the keys from the father to the daughter.

Talk about who, in addition to the father and daughter, might be present at this ceremony. Talk about the ritual actions that might be carried out and any ritualised words that might be spoken in the scene.

Take time to experiment with how this ceremony might take place. You may need to try out a variety of different ways before you find a format that you are satisfied with. You may wish to use some of the words from the inscriptions and scrolls as part of the ceremony.

Remember that the father is holding Portia to a promise not to reveal the contents of the caskets to any of the suitors.

Show your version of the ceremonial handing over of the caskets to the daughter and the announcement of their significance in terms of the daughter's marriage partner.

Discuss the ritual elements that appeared in each of the group's work and their significance.

Write the script for your handing-over ceremony in your logbook.

❋ *Had you been as wise as bold*

You are now going to engage in a hot seat activity. A hot seat is a situation where one character is questioned by others. The questions usually explore the feelings and motivations of the character.

Each student who played the part of the daughter, Portia, in the ritual improvisation should take it in turn to sit in the hot seat. The remainder of the class will ask questions of each of the Portias about their feelings towards the father and his will.

Think carefully about the questions you could ask each Portia about the type of man she would like to marry and what her chances of marrying this type of man might be given the casket lottery that her father has set up with his will. You may wish to explore her feelings about her father. Does she doubt the wisdom of his decision?

After each Portia has had a turn in the hot seat, discuss the issues that have been raised.

Imagine that you are a reporter who has interviewed this wealthy heiress about her father's will and the conditions placed upon her future husband. Write the story for your newspaper or magazine. Think about your audience and the kind of story that they will want to hear and shape the information that you received from the interview in the hot seat so that they will enjoy the story.

Publish your story for others in the class to read.

❋ *I would not lose you*

The following lines come from Portia's speeches in the play. Work with a small group. Read the lines aloud and experiment with ways of saying them to communicate the feelings that Portia might have for Bassanio.

PORTIA   I pray you tarry, pause a day or two
                 Before you hazard, for in choosing wrong
                 I lose your company.

                 There's something tells me, but it is not love,
                 I would not lose you.

I would detain you here some month or two
Before you venture for me. I could teach you
How to choose right, but then I am forsworn.

One half of me is yours, the other half yours –
Mine own I would say: but if mine then yours,
And so all yours.

If you do love me, you will find me out.

You see me, Lord Bassanio, where I stand,
Such as I am. Though for myself alone
I would not be ambitious in my wish
To wish myself much better, yet for you
I would be trebled twenty times myself,
A thousand times more fair, ten thousand times
More rich, that only to stand high in your account,
I might in virtues, beauties, livings, friends,
Exceed account. But the full sum of me
Is sum of something: which to term in gross
Is an unlessoned girl, unschooled, unpractised;
Happy in this, she is not yet so old
But she may learn; happier than this,
She is not bred so dull but she can learn;
Happiest of all, is that her gentle spirit
Commits itself to yours to be directed
As from her lord, her governor, her king.

Work in groups. Each group should create a voice collage that expresses Portia's feelings for Bassanio. You may wish to use some of Portia's words and any other words you need to create the collage. You may also wish to include some vocal sounds that are not words.

When you have rehearsed your collage, present it to the other groups.

Spend some time discussing the effects of these collages in creating the character of Portia.

Write the script for this collage scene in your logbook.

❋ *He is little better than a beast*

There were many suitors who came to woo Portia, but not all of these went through the ritual choosing of the caskets. Some of these suitors are mentioned in Act 1 Scene 2. Below you will find some of these suitors as Portia describes them to Nerissa in that scene. There may also have been other suitors who are not mentioned in this scene.

Work in small groups. Read through the following descriptions of these suitors.

Neapolitan Prince – that's a colt indeed, for he doth nothing but talk of his horse; and he makes it a great appropriation to his own good parts that he can shoe him himself.

County Palatine – he doth nothing but frown, as who should say, 'And you will not have me, choose.' He hears merry tales and smiles not; I fear he will prove the weeping philosopher when he grows old, being so full of unmannerly sadness in his youth.

Monsieur le Bon – he hath a horse better than the Neapolitan's, a better bad habit of frowning than the Count Palatine: he is every man in no man. If a throstle sing, he falls straight a-capering; he will fence with his own shadow.

Falconbridge, young baron of England – he hath neither Latin, French, nor Italian. He is a proper man's picture, but alas who can converse with a dumbshow? How oddly he is suited! I think he bought his doublet in Italy, his round hose in France, his bonnet in Germany, and his behaviour everywhere.

The Scottish lord – he borrowed a box of the ear of the Englishman and swore he would pay him again when he was able.

The Duke of Saxony's nephew – very vile in the morning when he is sober, and most vile in the afternoon when he is drunk. When he is best he is a little worse than a man, and when he is worst he is little better than a beast.

Discuss your impressions of these suitors and their motivations in seeking Portia's hand in marriage. If these are typical of the suitors coming to woo Portia, was her father perhaps wise to take the action with the caskets? Or is Portia capable of making sensible decisions about men?

Write your ideas in your logbook.

✳ *A colt indeed*

Work with a partner. Set up a sculptured pose for one of the suitors described by Portia. Or alternatively, adopt a pose for another suitor of your own imagining. Take time to experiment with your sculptured poses.

Share your poses with the rest of the class. Discuss the kind of person each one is, and speculate as to whether he would make a suitable husband for Portia.

Can you imagine why Portia's father might have included the condition in his will that prevents Portia from marrying without the trial by casket?

Write your ideas in your logbook.

✳ *Every man in no man*

Consider how the suitor that you have sculpted might walk and move. Experiment with movements and walks until you are satisfied with the character that you have constructed.

Work as a whole class. You are now going to set up an improvised scene with one student playing Portia. The three caskets should be set out before Portia.

In this improvised scene each suitor will walk in, survey the caskets one by one and walk out. The actor playing Portia will face the audience throughout the scene as each suitor comes in and looks at the caskets.

Portia will convey her feelings about each character through her facial expression and through any appropriate gestures or body language. In this scene no words will be spoken, so the actions, walks, facial expressions, gestures and body language must express what each character is feeling. This scene will have similar effects to the ritual scene that you constructed earlier.

The chosen suitors should complete this action without interruption. Afterwards the audience should discuss the scene, commenting on the feelings that Portia expressed through her body language, gestures and facial expressions.

Record this action in your logbook.

※ *Where is fancy bred?*

Work in small groups and talk about the kind of music which could accompany this scene as each of the suitors looks at the caskets. Experiment with improvising music and exploring music from recorded sources. Replay the scene with different kinds of music and discuss how the choice of music changes the meaning of the scene.

Write your observations in your logbook. Record an outline of this scenario in your logbook.

※ *In the heart, or in the head?*

The following words are from the song which is sung during the casket scene in the play while Bassanio makes his choice of casket.

> Tell me where is fancy bred,
> Or in the heart, or in the head?
> How begot, how nourishèd?
> Reply, reply.
> It is engend'red in the eye,
> With gazing fed, and fancy dies
> In the cradle where it lies.
> Let us all ring fancy's knell.
> I'll begin it – Ding, dong, bell.
> Ding, dong, bell.

Work in groups. Talk about the lyrics of this song. What dramatic effect does it have at this point in the scene? Each group should improvise the music for, or compose a tune for, this song. Decide on which suitor the song will be sung for. Consider carefully the implications of the song as the suitor is perusing the caskets. Are there hints in the words of the song that could be picked up by the suitor if he listens carefully?

Take time to experiment with the words and music to develop a suitable mood for the particular suitor. Experiment with how the song would sound for Arragon and how this might differ for Morocco, for instance.

When you have experimented with music, replay the scene that you developed with the suitors, using the song as musical background. You may need to adjust the rhythm and pace of the music to fit the walk and movement of each character.

The audience should discuss the effects of this music on the meaning of the scene. Consider particularly the repetition of the words and the effect that this has on the audience's view of the character of the suitor.

Record your explorations and discoveries in your logbook.

✳ *Some god direct my judgement*

There are three main characters in the play who do elect to undertake the ritual of the casket-choosing – Morocco, Arragon and Bassanio.

Work in large groups. There should be three groups in the class. Each group should take one of these characters. Each group is to devise two still images. The first still image should show the moment when the character makes the decision about which casket he will choose. The second still image should show the moment of realisation as he opens the casket and perceives that he has chosen the wrong casket, in the case of Morocco and Arragon, and the correct casket in the case of Bassanio. Some members of the group may wish to direct these images.

Spend some time exploring these moments of decision and realisation. Think about who else is present at this moment and how each one might react.

Take time to explore and develop your images and then present them to the rest of the class. Ask the audience to provide feedback on their impressions. Ask the audience to consider how the dramatic tension could be increased in these two key moments. Experiment with the ideas that the audience suggests to heighten the dramatic tension.

Write your ideas in your logbook.

✳ *Weigh thy value with an even hand*

You are now going to repeat the still images, but this time you are going to use a freeze-dissolve-freeze technique. You will first establish the freeze for the moment of choice, and then move in very slow motion from this first still image into the second still image and then hold the freeze in this second image. Take time to rework your image for this presentation. Be sure to move very slowly between the two images.

Present your freeze-dissolve-freeze to the others in the class. Encourage the audience to discuss the images and ideas that this technique highlights.

Write down your impressions of the three characters who woo Portia and make the casket choice. To what extent does their choice of the caskets reveal their characters?

Write your ideas in your logbook.

❋ *I am enjoined by oath*

You are now going to play this scene incorporating some improvised dialogue. Each group should consider who might speak in the scene and what they might say. The main focus in these scenes is on the choice of the caskets and their contents. Consider how the character might approach the task. This is also a ritualised scene and the dialogue should also contain some elements of ritual.

Take time to experiment. Present your improvised scene to the rest of the class. Discuss the dialogue that each group has used.

Read the following segments of dialogue from the play as written by Shakespeare. Try reading the dialogue aloud. Revisit your improvisations and experiment with incorporating some of the lines from Shakespeare's play within your own improvisation.

MOROCCO (*before choosing*)

> Some god direct my judgement! Let me see:
> I will survey th'inscriptions back again.
> What says this leaden casket?
> 'Who chooseth me, must give and hazard all he hath.'
> Must give – for what? For lead? Hazard for lead!
> This casket threatens: men that hazard all
> Do it in hope of fair advantages.
> A golden mind stoops not to shows of dross;
> I'll then nor give nor hazard aught for lead.
> What says the silver with her virgin hue?
> 'Who chooseth me, shall get as much as he deserves.'
> As much as he deserves – pause there, Morocco,
> And weigh thy value with an even hand.
> If thou be'st rated by thy estimation
> Thou dost deserve enough; and yet enough
> May not extend so far as to the lady;
> And yet to be afeared of my deserving
> Were but a weak disabling of myself.
> As much as I deserve: why, that's the lady.
> I do in birth deserve her, and in fortunes,
> In graces, and in qualities of breeding:
> But more than these, in love I do deserve.
> What if I strayed no farther, but chose here?

Let's see once more this saying graved in gold:
'Who chooseth me, shall gain what many men desire.'
Why, that's the lady; all the world desires her.
From the four corners of the earth they come
To kiss this shrine, this mortal breathing saint.
The Hyrcanian deserts and the vasty wilds
Of wide Arabia are as throughfares now
For princes to come view fair Portia.
The watery kingdom, whose ambitious head
Spits in the face of heaven, is no bar
To stop the foreign spirits, but they come
As o'er a brook to see fair Portia.
One of these three contains her heavenly picture.
Is't like that lead contains her? 'Twere damnation
To think so base a thought; it were too gross
To rib her cerecloth in the òbscure grave.
Or shall I think in silver she's immured,
Being ten times undervalued to tried gold?
O sinful thought! Never so rich a gem
Was set in worse than gold. They have in England
A coin that bears the figure of an angel
Stampèd in gold; but that's insculped upon:
But here an angel in a golden bed
Lies all within. Deliver me the key:
Here do I choose and thrive I as I may.

MOROCCO (*after choosing*)
                O hell! What have we here?
A carrion death, within whose empty eye
There is a written scroll.

ARRAGON (*before choosing*)
I am enjoined by oath to observe three things:
First, never to unfold to anyone
Which casket 'twas I chose; next, if I fail
Of the right casket, never in my life
To woo a maid in way of marriage; lastly,
If I do fail in fortune of my choice,
Immediately to leave you and be gone.
And so have I addressed me. Fortune now
To my heart's hope! Gold, silver, and base lead.
'Who chooseth me, must give and hazard all he hath.'
You shall look fairer ere I give or hazard.
What says the golden chest? Ha, let me see:
'Who chooseth me, shall gain what many men desire.'
What many men desire; that 'many' may be meant

By the fool multitude that choose by show,
Not learning more than the fond eye doth teach,
Which pries not to th'interior, but like the martlet
Builds in the weather on the outward wall,
Even in the force and road of casualty.
I will not choose what many men desire,
Because I will not jump with common spirits
And rank me with the barbarous multitudes.
Why then, to thee, thou silver treasure house:
Tell me once more what title thou dost bear.
'Who chooseth me, shall get as much as he deserves.'
And well said too, for who shall go about
To cozen Fortune and be honourable
Without the stamp of merit? Let none presume
To wear an undeservèd dignity.
O, that estates, degrees, and offices
Were not derived corruptly, and that clear honour
Were purchased by the merit of the wearer!
How many then should cover that stand bare!
How many be commanded that command!
How much low peasantry would then be gleaned
From the true seed of honour, and how much honour
Picked from the chaff and ruin of the times
To be new varnished! Well, but to my choice.
'Who chooseth me, shall get as much as he deserves.'
I will assume desert. Give me a key for this,
And instantly unlock my fortunes here.

ARRAGON (*after choosing*)
What's here? The portrait of a blinking idiot
Presenting me a schedule! I will read it.
How much unlike art thou to Portia!
How much unlike my hopes and my deservings.
'Who chooseth me, shall have as much as he deserves.'
Did I deserve no more than a fool's head?
Is that my prize? Are my deserts no better?

BASSANIO (*before choosing*)
So may the outward shows be least themselves:
The world is still deceived with ornament.
In law, what plea so tainted and corrupt
But, being seasoned with a gracious voice,
Obscures the show of evil? In religion,
What damnèd error but some sober brow
Will bless it and approve it with a text,
Hiding the grossness with fair ornament?

There is no vice so simple but assumes
Some mark of virtue on his outward parts.
How many cowards whose hearts are all as false
As stayers of sand, wear yet upon their chins
The beards of Hercules and frowning Mars,
Who inward searched have livers white as milk,
And these assume but valour's excrement
To render them redoubted. Look on beauty,
And you shall see 'tis purchased by the weight,
Which therein works a miracle in nature,
Making them lightest that wear most of it.
So are those crispèd snaky golden locks
Which maketh such wanton gambols with the wind
Upon supposèd fairness, often known
To be the dowry of a second head,
The skull that bred them in the sepulchre.
Thus ornament is but the guilèd shore
To a most dangerous sea; the beauteous scarf
Veiling an Indian beauty; in a word,
The seeming truth which cunning times put on
To entrap the wisest. Therefore thou gaudy gold,
Hard food for Midas, I will none of thee,
Nor none of thee, thou pale and common drudge
'Tween man and man. But thou, thou meagre lead
Which rather threaten'st than dost promise aught,
Thy paleness moves me more than eloquence:
And here choose I. Joy be the consequence!

BASSANIO (*after choosing*)
                    What find I here?
Fair Portia's counterfeit! What demigod
Hath come so near creation? Move those eyes?
Or whether riding on the balls of mine
Seem they in motion? Here are severed lips
Parted with sugar breath; so sweet a bar
Should sunder such sweet friends. Here in her hairs
The painter plays the spider, and hath woven
A golden mesh t'entrap the hearts of men
Faster than gnats in cobwebs. But her eyes –
How could he see to do them? Having made one,
Methinks it should have power to steal both his
And leave itself unfurnished. Yet look how far
The substance of my praise doth wrong this shadow
In underprizing it, so far this shadow
Doth limp behind the substance. Here's the scroll,
The continent and summary of my fortune.

A gentle scroll! Fair lady, by your leave.
I come by note to give, and to receive.
Like one of two contending in a prize
That thinks he hath done well in people's eyes,
Hearing applause and universal shout,
Giddy in spirit, still gazing in a doubt
Whether those peals of praise be his or no –
So, thrice-fair lady, stand I even so,
As doubtful whether what I see be true,
Until confirmed, signed, ratified by you.

Record your impressions in your logbook.

❀ *What find I here?*

You are now going to experiment with another exercise that enables you to explore what a character is thinking and feeling. The alter ego is the other 'I', the voice that runs inside our heads, that does not necessarily express what we are thinking and feeling to the outside world.

Work in small groups. Select one member of the group to play the part of Portia and another to play the part of Portia's alter ego. This alter ego stands behind Portia on the stage and speaks directly to the audience.

Now replay the scenes that you have developed in which the suitors come to choose the caskets. As the suitors talk to Portia have them pause and allow time for Portia's alter ego to comment to the audience on the actions of the suitors. The alter ego will tell the audience what Portia is thinking or feeling – something that she, the real Portia, cannot do in front of the suitors.

Show your version of this alter ego scene to other groups in the class. Discuss the effects of this technique on the audience's perception of the suitor and the audience's perception of Portia.

You may wish to repeat this alter ego exercise using an alter ego for the suitor.

Record your observations and discoveries in your logbook.

❀ *The seeming truth*

Shakespeare often used a technique called 'aside'. This technique is rather like the alter ego exercise that you have just completed. In asides, a character speaks directly to the audience telling them what that character really thinks about the other characters and their actions. Shakespeare made considerable use of this stage device when he wanted the audience to have a different perspective on the action.

Write the script for your scene using this device of aside where appropriate, incorporating comments that the alter ego has made in the improvisations.

✳ *Joy be the consequence*

Many of Shakespeare's plays ended with a dance. Work in groups. Each group should improvise or choreograph a dance that would express the mood of Bassanio's successful selection of the casket containing Portia's portrait.

Take time to select music and to experiment with choreography. Have groups share their versions of the dance.

Record your choreography in your logbook.

✳ *You will find me out*

Shakespeare wrote his plays in a poetic form called 'blank verse'. Consult chapter 1 for further information on Shakespeare's use of blank verse.

In speaking the lines from the play, the actor needs to read to the end of the line where the primary stressed word usually occurs.

Read the following lines, listening for the rhythm and beat of the lines and reading to the end of the line to find the primary stress. Note any regular or irregular patterns. Experiment with these patterns. You may wish to consult chapter 1 for further information about speaking these lines.

PORTIA   Away then! I am locked in one of them:
If you do love me, you will find me out.
Nerissa and the rest, stand all aloof.
Let music sound while he doth make his choice;
Then if he lose he makes a swan-like end,
Fading in music. That the comparison
May stand more proper, my eye shall be the stream
And watery deathbed for him. He may win,
And what is music then? Then music is
Even as the flourish when true subjects bow
To a new-crownèd monarch. Such it is
As are those dulcet sounds in break of day,
That creep into the dreaming bridegroom's ear
And summon him to marriage. Now he goes

With no less presence, but with much more love,
Than young Alcides when he did redeem
The virgin tribute paid by howling Troy
To the sea-monster. I stand for sacrifice.
The rest aloof are the Dardanian wives,
With bleared visages come forth to view
The issue of th'exploit. Go, Hercules!
Live thou, I live. With much much more dismay
I view the fight than thou that mak'st the fray.

❋ Building the play

You are now going to build your own play from these explorations. You may
wish to discuss which scenes to use and the order in which they could occur
in the playbuilt play. Alternatively, you may wish to use the following order
for your play:

• the death bed – Portia's father hands over the will and the caskets
• verbal collage – Portia expresses her feelings about her situation
• parade of suitors with Portia's asides
• Morocco chooses the gold casket
• parade of suitors with Portia's asides
• Arragon chooses the silver casket
• parade of suitors with Portia's asides
• Bassanio chooses the lead casket
• celebration dance.

Casting

You may wish to cast the roles for performance. You will need to cast the key
roles of Portia, Bassanio, Arragon and Morocco. In addition, you may need
to cast other suitors for the parade scene, voices for the collage scene, and the
dance finale and any other scenes you have incorporated. You may also wish
to include other moments from your improvised scenes to build up the play.

Rehearsing scenes

Revisit the scenes that you developed throughout the playbuilding process,
tightening up any timing or movement. Work on speech if necessary. You will
need to rehearse the timing of action and the speeches, particularly any where
you have incorporated lines from Shakespeare's play.

Linking scenes

When all the individual scenes are well rehearsed, have a complete run-through of this playbuilt play. Shakespeare did not have breaks between scenes, and one scene flowed into the next without pause. You should attempt to do the same.

Consider whether any links other than music are necessary between the scenes. Consider whether you could leave Portia's father on the stage after the first scene and what effect this might have for the audience's understanding of the power of the will of a dead father.

Performing

When you have thoroughly rehearsed the play, present it to an audience and encourage the audience members to give you feedback on their responses to the play.

You may wish to develop a printed program that provides your audience with information that you have explored throughout the playbuilding process.

Write your own responses to the play and the playbuilding process in your journal. Keep a copy of the final script that you used for your performance.

When you have presented your version of the casket story, you may wish to explore the rest of Shakespeare's play, *The Merchant of Venice*. The Cambridge School Shakespeare edition provides further suggestions for workshop activities for each scene in the play.

The Ides of March

Julius Caesar

In this unit you will be exploring the story from one of Shakespeare's historical plays – *Julius Caesar*. You will build a version of the story that uses your own ideas as well as some of the scenes from Shakespeare's play.

✳ *Preliminary discussion*

The play *Julius Caesar* draws upon real historical events, but it is not an attempt to present these in a documentary fashion. Rather the play builds on the events and makes statements about power, manipulation, revenge, ambition and friendship. It is also intrinsically concerned with the great existential question – who controls our destiny?

Work with a small group. Do some research to find out about Julius Caesar and the life and times of the Roman Empire. Present your research to the rest of the class in the format of a *Julius Caesar – This is Your Life* television program.

Spend some time talking about the ideas and issues that have arisen in your research. Record your information in your logbook.

✿ *We make holiday to see Caesar*

Work in small groups. Do some research to find out about the Roman feast of Lupercal. How would you present this feast with its celebratory processions on a stage?

Work with a large group to create a tableau that would show Caesar celebrating his return to Rome in a procession past all the citizens of Rome at the feast of Lupercal. How do the citizens of Rome show their feelings about this triumphal return to Rome? How does the atmosphere of the feast of Lupercal affect this triumphal return?

Create a soundscape that could show the feelings of the crowd.

Write your ideas in your logbook.

✿ *The Ides of March*

A soothsayer or fortune teller is central to the opening action of the play. The Soothsayer makes a prediction about the Ides of March (March 15). Working in a group, create a sculpture of the Soothsayer using one member of the group as the Soothsayer, and the others contributing to the sculptured form. Talk about the kind of person you have created. Why did you choose that particular physical form? What image of the Soothsayer does this project to the audience?

Work in small groups and talk about how you would feel if you were told by this Soothsayer that you should be wary of a particular day in March. How would you react? What difference do you think it would make if you were a very powerful and successful person?

Record your ideas in your logbook.

✿ *Beware*

Work in a large group. You are going to improvise a scene with Caesar and the Soothsayer. Have one person in the group take on the role of Caesar. Sculpt him as a strong, successful and powerful leader. Have the others in the group take roles as Caesar's followers. Have the Soothsayer approach the group and call out to Caesar over the noise of the others. The Soothsayer can only speak this one line, although, of course, he may say it more than once.

Beware the Ides of March.

When you have completed your improvisation, talk about what happened in the scene. What did it reveal about Caesar as a leader? What words would you use to describe Caesar? Who else spoke in the improvisation? What did they reveal about their relationships with Caesar?

Now repeat the improvisation, the Soothsayer may again only speak the one line. The scene, however, must end this time with Caesar speaking this line:

> He is a dreamer; let us leave him.

Reposition this improvised scene in the tableau which you have created of the crowd welcoming Caesar. How does this alter the meaning of the tableau?

Record your impressions in your logbook.

✳ Yond Cassius has a lean and hungry look

Read the following edited version of a monologue that Caesar delivers. Talk about what Caesar is feeling at this point in time. Notice that this speech is in blank verse. You may wish to refer to chapter 1 for further information about blank verse.

CAESAR
Yond Cassius has a lean and hungry look,
He thinks too much: such men are dangerous.
He is a great observer, and he looks
Quite through the deeds of men. He loves no plays,
         he hears no music;
Seldom he smiles, and smiles in such a sort
As if he mocked himself and scorned his spirit
That could be moved to smile at any thing.
Such men as he be never at heart's ease
Whiles they behold a greater than themselves,
And therefore are they very dangerous.
I rather tell thee what is to be feared
Than what I fear: for always I am Caesar.

Create a second tableau which shows that the procession has moved on. Position one character, Cassius, at a distance from the procession.

While the tableau is held, have the character of Caesar step out of the tableau and speak some or all of these lines directly to the audience.

Share this scene with other groups. What issues are raised by this scene?

Create a further tableau which shows the departure of the procession, leaving behind Cassius and Brutus. Imagine that both of these characters are able to express their feelings in an improvised soliloquy to the audience. Neither character can hear what the other says, as each is standing in the tableau. Spend some time talking about the impressions that you now have of these characters.

Record these improvised soliloquies in your logbook.

✼ Noble Brutus

Work with a partner. One of you should take on the role of Brutus and the other should take on the role of Cassius. Both have been part of the crowd scene and have observed Caesar and the Soothsayer and the reactions of the crowd of followers. Neither is particularly pleased. The crowd has moved on and these two stay behind.

Improvise the conversation that these two men might exchange after the others have disappeared. You may wish to experiment with a number of possible duologue conversations until you are satisfied with the results. Share your duologue with others and talk about the scenes that you have created.

Record the dialogue in your logbook.

✼ What means this shouting?

While Brutus and Cassius are continuing their duologue, two moments of shouting and blowing of trumpets are heard offstage.

Work with a group. Two of you should take on the role of Brutus and Cassius, and two should be their alter egos. The rest should take on the role of the citizens who are offstage cheering Caesar.

Read through the sections of the scene printed below. The actors playing Brutus and Cassius should pause after each speech to allow their alter egos to comment directly to the audience.

Flourish and shout

BRUTUS	What means this shouting? I do fear the people Choose Caesar for their king.
CASSIUS	Ay, do you fear it? Then must I think you would not have it so.
BRUTUS	I would not, Cassius, yet I love him well. But wherefore do you hold me here so long? What is it that you would impart to me?
CASSIUS	I cannot tell what you and other men Think of this life, but for my single self I had as lief not be as live to be In awe of such a thing as I myself.

I was born free as Caesar, so were you;
We both have fed as well, and we can both
Endure the winter's cold as well as he.
          And this man
Is now become a god, and Cassius is
A wretched creature and must bend his body
If Caesar carelessly but nod on him.
          Ye gods, it doth amaze me
A man of such a feeble temper should
So get the start of the majestic world
And bear the palm alone.

Shout. Flourish

BRUTUS   Another general shout!
I do believe that these applauses are
For some new honours that are heaped on Caesar.

CASSIUS   Why, man, he doth bestride the narrow world
Like a Colossus, and we petty men
Walk under his huge legs and peep about
To find ourselves dishonourable graves.
Men at some time are masters of their fates:
The fault, dear Brutus, is not in our stars
But in ourselves, that we are underlings.
Brutus and Caesar: what should be in that 'Caesar'?
Why should that name be sounded more than yours?
Now in the names of all the gods at once,
Upon what meat doth this our great Caesar feed
That he is grown so great? Age, thou art shamed!
Rome, thou hast lost the breed of noble bloods!
When could they say, till now, that talked of Rome,
That her wide walks encompassed but one man?

BRUTUS   That you do love me, I am nothing jealous;
What you would work me to, I have some aim.
How I have thought of this, and of these times,
I shall recount hereafter. What you have said
I will consider; what you have to say
I will with patience hear and find a time
Both meet to hear and answer such high things.
Till then, my noble friend, chew upon this:
Brutus had rather be a villager
Than to repute himself a son of Rome
Under these hard conditions as this time
Is like to lay upon us.

CASSIUS	I am glad that my weak words Have struck but thus much show of fire from Brutus.
BRUTUS	Tomorrow if you please to speak with me, I will come home to you; or if you will, Come home to me and I will wait for you.
CASSIUS	I will do so. Till then, think of the world.

Spend some time talking about these two characters and their inner feelings. Rehearse the scene again without the alter egos, but showing, through the characters' movements, positioning and speech, the inner thoughts and feelings at each stage of the duologue.

Record your impressions of these characters in your logbook.

❋ *Thou art noble*

Work with a partner. Read through the soliloquy printed below. Talk about Cassius' motives in engaging Brutus in this conspiracy. What is your impression of Brutus from this encounter and from Cassius' speech?

CASSIUS	Well, Brutus, thou art noble; yet I see Thy honourable metal may be wrought From that it is disposed. Therefore it is meet That noble minds keep ever with their likes; For who so firm that cannot be seduced? Caesar doth bear me hard, but he loves Brutus. If I were Brutus now and he were Cassius, He should not humour me.

Replay the last scene and add in this soliloquy after Brutus has left. Record this action in your logbook.

❋ *The rabblement hooted*

Casca followed the procession to the Capitol and observed the events there. He reports on these events to Cassius and Brutus.

Work in a large group. Read through the recount of the events. Talk about how this happened. What do you think Cicero might have said in Greek?

I saw Mark Antony offer Caesar a crown – yet 'twas not a crown neither, 'twas one of these coronets – and he put it by once; but for all that, to my thinking he would fain have had it. Then he offered it to him again; then he put it by again; but to my thinking he was very loath to lay his fingers off it. And then he offered it the third time; he put it the third time by, and still as he refused it, the rabblement hooted, and clapped their chopped hands, and threw their sweaty nightcaps, and uttered such a deal of stinking breath because Caesar refused the crown that it had, almost, choked Caesar, for he swounded and fell down at it. He fell down in the market-place, and foamed at the mouth, and was speechless. The tag-rag people did not clap him and hiss him according as he pleased and displeased them, as they use to do the players in the theatre. When he perceived the common herd was glad he refused the crown, he plucked ope his doublet and offered them his throat to cut. And so he fell. When he came to himself again, he said if he had done or said anything amiss, he desired their worships to think it was his infirmity. Three of four wenches cried, 'Alas, good soul', and forgave him with all their hearts. But there's not heed to be taken of them. Cicero spoke Greek and those that understood him smiled at one another and shook their heads.

Improvise a dumbshow scene that enacts the events which Casca describes. Consider how Caesar put the crown aside on each occasion. Experiment with the swooning, and the sounds of the crowd.

Show your dumbshow version of the scene to other groups in the class. Have one person read the lines as a voice-over for the dumbshow scene. Talk about the ideas that these scenes communicate.

Record your impressions in your logbook.

✳ *They are portentous things*

The next phase of the conspiracy occurs against a background of violent storms and unnatural events. It is the eve of the Ides of March. In Shakespeare's theatre there was little technology that could evoke the scene with its violent tempest. Shakespeare had to create this mood through his words and the actions and gestures of the players.

Work in a small group. Read through the description that Casca gives of the tempest and the strange events that occurred. Explore how you might present this without the words. Could you use sound, music, visual images, movement, dance?

CASCA   ...all the sway of earth
                          Shakes like a thing unfirm?
                          I have seen tempests when the scolding winds
                          Have rived the knotty oaks, and I have seen
                          Th'ambitious ocean swell, and rage, and foam,
                          To be exalted with the threatening clouds;
                          But never till tonight, never till now,
                          Did I go through a tempest dropping fire.

> A common slave
> Held up his left hand, which did flame and burn
> Like twenty torches joined, and yet his hand,
> Not sensible of fire, remained unscorched.
> Against the Capitol I met a lion
> Who glazed upon me and went surly by
> Without annoying me. And there were drawn
> Upon a heap a hundred ghastly women,
> Transformèd with their fear, who swore they saw
> Men, all in fire, walk up and down the streets.
> And yesterday the bird of night did sit
> Even at noon-day upon the market-place,
> Hooting and shrieking.

Construct a soundscape that communicates this mood. You may wish to supplement the soundscape with visual images, either projected on to a screen, or enacted through movement. Show your scene to other groups and discuss the moods created by each.

Record a description of this scene in your logbook.

❋ *He shall wear his crown*

Cassius' next action is to tie all the conspirators into an agreement. He does this one by one, persuading them to join in what he convinces them is a worthwhile and noble deed. Work with a partner. One of you should take on the role of Cassius and one of Casca. Read through the following edited version of this scene.

CASCA	Who ever knew the heavens menace so?
CASSIUS	Those that have known the earth so full of faults.
CASCA	It is the part of men to fear and tremble When the most mighty gods by tokens send Such dreadful heralds to astonish us.
CASSIUS	Now could I, Casca, name to thee a man Most like this dreadful night, That thunders, lightens, opens graves, and roars As doth the lion in the Capitol – A man no mightier than thyself, or me, In personal action, yet prodigious grown And fearful, as these strange eruptions are.
CASCA	'Tis Caesar that you mean?
CASSIUS	Let it be who it is, for Romans now Have thews and limbs like their ancestors'.

But, woe the while, our fathers' minds are dead
And we are governed with our mothers' spirits.

CASCA   Indeed, they say the senators tomorrow
Mean to establish Caesar as a king,
And he shall wear his crown by sea and land.

CASSIUS   I know where I will wear this dagger then.
Therein, ye gods, you make the weak most strong;
Therein, ye gods, you tyrants do defeat.
That part of tyranny that I do bear
I can shake off at pleasure.

CASCA   　　　　　　　　So can I,
So every bondman in his own hand bears
The power to cancel his captivity.

CASSIUS   Those that with haste will make a mighty fire
Begin it with weak straws. What trash is Rome,
What rubbish and what offal, when it serves
For the base matter to illuminate
So vile a thing as Caesar? But, O grief,
Where hast thou led me? I perhaps speak this
Before a willing bondman.

CASCA   You speak to Casca, and to such a man
That is no fleering tell-tale. Hold, my hand.

CASSIUS   　　　　　　　There's a bargain made.
Come, Casca, you and I will yet, ere day,
See Brutus at his house. Three parts of him
Is ours already, and the man entire
Upon the next encounter yields him ours.

CASCA   O, he sits high in all the people's hearts,
And that which would appear offence in us
His countenance, like richest alchemy,
Will change to virtue and to worthiness.

CASSIUS   Him and his worth and our great need of him
You have right well conceited. Let us go.

Talk about the way that Cassius manipulates Casca. Discuss your impressions of Casca. Using some of the lines, develop an improvised scene that shows how Cassius wins Casca over to his conspiracy.

Rehearse your version and then show it to others in the class.

Improvise similar scenes that show how Cassius wins over the other conspirators: Decius, Cinna, Metellus Cimber, Trebonius.

Record your version in your logbook.

✳ *It must be by his death*

Brutus is an honourable man who wants to do the right thing. He thinks through the situation, carefully weighing up the arguments. The soliloquy that he speaks at this point in the play shows the torment in his mind as he has to make up his mind about the conspiracy.

Work in groups. One person should take on the role of Brutus, and the other people should become the chorus which speaks his inner thoughts. Brutus should be in the centre of the playing space. Each thought should be spoken to Brutus, who must listen carefully and respond through facial expression, movement, gesture and words that echo the words thrown to him.

BRUTUS   It must be by his death.

           And for my part
I know no personal cause to spurn at him
But for the general.
         He would be crowned:
How that might change his nature, there's the question.
It is the bright day that brings forth the adder
And that craves wary walking.
            Crown him that,
And then I grant we put a sting in him
That at his will he may do danger with.
Th'abuse of greatness is when it disjoins
Remorse from power.
         And to speak truth of Caesar,
I have not known when his affections swayed
More than his reason.
         But 'tis a common proof
That lowliness is young ambition's ladder,
Whereto the climber-upward turns his face;
He then unto the ladder turns his back,
Looks in the clouds, scorning the base degrees
By which he did ascend.
         So Caesar may.
Then lest he may, prevent.
         And since the quarrel
Will bear no colour for the thing he is,
Fashion it thus:
       that what he is, augmented,
Would run to these and these extremities.
And therefore think him as a serpent's egg
(Which, hatched, would as his kind, grow mischievous)
And kill him in the shell.

Since Cassius first did whet me against Caesar
I have not slept.

Between the acting of a dreadful thing
And the first motion, all the interim is
Like a phantasma or a hideous dream.
The genius and the mortal instruments
Are then in council, and the state of a man,
Like to a little kingdom, suffers then
The nature of an insurrection.

Record this scene in your logbook.

�֍ *Know I these men?*

Conspiracies are often arranged in secret. There is a ritual that goes with the sealing of a contract or conspiracy. Sometimes this is the shaking of hands, or other ritualised gestures.

The conspirators are: Brutus, Cassius, Casca, Decius, Cinna, Metellus Cimber, Trebonius.

Work in groups of seven. Experiment with ritual gestures, movements and facial expressions that could be used by these conspirators. Explore how they might stand or sit as a group, establishing the individual relationships between these people.

Improvise a wordless dumbshow scene in which Brutus receives the conspirators one by one, to form a group and seal the deal that will bind them as the murderers of Caesar.

Show your scene to others in the class. Talk about the issues that this scene raises.

Record the scene and your ideas about it in your logbook.

✖ *Our course will seem too bloody*

Continue to work in the same group. Improvise a scene using dialogue in which the conspirators discuss others who might be persuaded to join in the act, and others who should also be cut down or killed.

Talk about the way the group acted when names were suggested as either further conspirators or other victims.

Read through the following edited version of this scene from the play.

CASSIUS	Let us swear our resolution.
BRUTUS	No, not an oath! If not the face of men,
	The sufferance of our souls, the time's abuse –
	If these be motives weak, break off betimes,
	And every man hence to his idle bed;
	So let high-sighted tyranny range on,
	Till each man drop by lottery. Countrymen,
	What need we any spur but our own cause
	To prick us to redress? What other bond
	Than secret Romans that have spoke the word
	And will not palter? And what other oath
	Than honesty to honesty engaged
	That this shall be or we will fall for it?
	Unto bad causes swear
	Such creatures as men doubt. But do not stain
	The even virtue of our enterprise,

	To think that or our cause or our performance
	Did need an oath.
CASSIUS	But what of Cicero? Shall we sound him?
CASCA	Let us not leave him out.
CINNA	No, by no means.
METELLUS	O, let us have him, for his silver hairs
	Will purchase us a good opinion.
BRUTUS	O, name him not, let us not break with him;
	For he will never follow anything
	That other men begin.
CASSIUS	Then leave him out.
DECIUS	Shall no man else be touched but only Caesar?
CASSIUS	Decius, well urged. I think it is not meet
	Mark Antony, so well beloved of Caesar,
	Should outlive Caesar. We shall find of him
	A shrewd contriver: which to prevent,
	Let Antony and Caesar fall together.
BRUTUS	Our course will seem too bloody, Caius Cassius,
	To cut the head off and then hack the limbs,
	For Antony is but a limb of Caesar.
	Let's be sacrificers, but not butchers, Caius.
	We all stand up against the spirit of Caesar,
	And in the spirit of men there is no blood.
	O, that we then could come by Caesar's spirit
	And not dismember Caesar! But, alas,
	Caesar must bleed for it. And, gentle friends,
	Let's kill him boldly, but not wrathfully;
	Let's carve him as a dish fit for the gods,
	Not hew him as a carcass fit for hounds.
	And for Mark Antony, think not of him,
	For he can do no more than Caesar's arm
	When Caesar's head is off.
CASSIUS	Yet I fear him.
BRUTUS	Alas, good Cassius, do not think of him.
	If he love Caesar, all that he can do
	Is to himself – take thought and die for Caesar.
TREBONIUS	There is no fear in him, let him not die,
	For he will live and laugh at this hereafter.
CASSIUS	The morning comes upon's. We'll leave you, Brutus,
	And, friends, disperse yourselves, but all remember
	What you have said and show yourselves true Romans.

BRUTUS   Good gentlemen, look fresh and merrily:
                     Let not our looks put on our purposes,
                     But bear it as our Roman actors do,
                     With untired spirits and formal constancy.
                     And so good morrow to you every one.

Rehearse this scene. Explore ways of setting the mood of conspiracy.
Record your ideas in your logbook.

�֎ *I grant I am a woman*

Both Brutus and Caesar have wives who appear to be more in tune with what
is happening in the world than their husbands are at this point in time. The
following lines are taken from the speeches of Brutus' wife, Portia, and
Caesar's wife, Calpurnia.

Work in groups of four. Each should take on one of the following roles:
Brutus, Portia, Caesar, Calpurnia. Place Brutus on one side of the stage and
Caesar on the other. The two wives should circle them as they speak.
Experiment with intercutting the lines between the two women as they try to
persuade their husbands.

PORTIA   Y'have ungently, Brutus,
                     Stole from my bed;
                                         and yesternight at supper
                     You suddenly arose and walked about,
                     Musing and sighing, with your arms across,

                     And when I asked you what the matter was,
                     You stared upon me with ungentle looks.
                     And with an angry wafture of your hand
                     Gave sign for me to leave you.

                     I should not know you, Brutus. Dear my lord,
                     Make me acquainted with your cause of grief.

                     You have some sick offence within your mind,
                     Which by the right and virtue of my place
                     I ought to know of.
                                         And upon my knees
                     I charm you, by my once commended beauty,
                     By all your vows of love, and that great vow
                     Which did incorporate and make us one,
                     That you unfold to me, your self, your half,
                     Why you are heavy.

Within the bond of marriage, tell me, Brutus,
Is it excepted I should know no secrets
That appertain to you?

                    Am I your self
But, as it were, in sort or limitation,
To keep with you at meals, comfort your bed,
And talk to you sometimes?

                    If it be no more
Portia is Brutus' harlot, not his wife.

I grant I am a woman, but withal
A woman that Lord Brutus took to wife.
Tell me your counsels, I will not disclose 'em.

CALPURNIA   What mean you, Caesar, think you to walk forth?
You shall not stir out of your house today.

Caesar, I never stood on ceremonies,
Yet now they fright me.

                    There is one within,
Besides the things that we have heard and seen,
Recounts most horrid sights seen by the watch.

A lioness hath whelpèd in the streets,
And graves have yawned and yielded up their dead;

Fierce fiery warriors fight upon the clouds
In ranks and squadrons and right form of war,
Which drizzled blood upon the Capitol;

The noise of battle hurtled in the air,
Horses did neigh and dying men did groan,
And ghosts did shriek and squeal about the streets.

O Caesar, these things are beyond all use,
And I do fear them.

When beggars die there are no comets seen,
The heavens themselves blaze forth the death of princes.

                    Alas, my lord,
Your wisdom is consumed in confidence.
Do not go forth today.

                    Call it my fear
That keeps you in the house, and not your own.
Let me, upon my knee, prevail in this.

Talk about why Caesar accedes to Calpurnia's request and agrees to stay while Brutus does not acquiesce to Portia's request.

Record in your logbook the scene that you have enacted.

※ *Shall Caesar send a lie*

While Caesar was persuaded by Calpurnia not to go to the Capitol, he soon changes his mind when confronted by Decius and his facile explanations and manipulations.

Work in groups of three. One should take on the role of Caesar, one should take on the role of Calpurnia and the third should take on the role of Decius. Read through the edited version of Caesar's speech printed below, and then improvise a scene in which Decius is able to persuade Caesar to change his mind.

CAESAR
> And you are come in very happy time
> To bear my greeting to the senators
> And tell them that I will not come today.
> The cause is in my will. I will not come:
> That is enough to satisfy the Senate.
> Calpurnia here, my wife, stays me at home.
> She dreamt tonight she saw my statue,
> Which like a fountain with an hundred spouts
> Did run pure blood and many lusty Romans
> Came smiling and did bathe their hands in it.
> And these does she apply for warnings and portents
> And evils imminent, and on her knee
> Hath begged that I will stay at home today.

Share your improvisation with other groups. Talk about how Decius managed to persuade Caesar that this dream was not an evil portent. What inducement did Decius give to persuade Caesar to go to the Capitol?

Replay your improvisation using the following lines for Decius.

DECIUS
>   The Senate have concluded
> To give this day a crown to mighty Caesar.
> If you shall send them word you will not come,
> Their minds may change.
>
> If Caesar hide himself, shall they not whisper,
> 'Lo, Caesar is afraid'?

What role did Calpurnia play in the scene? Although Calpurnia is present throughout the scene in Shakespeare's play she does not speak. Rework your improvisation so that Calpurnia is silent. Discuss the impression that this gives of her role as Caesar's wife. Repeat the improvisation. This time include as Caesar's last words:

CAESAR   How foolish do your fears seem now, Calpurnia!
                I am ashamèd I did yield to them.
                Give me my robe, for I will go.

Allow Calpurnia to speak an aside or soliloquy directly to the audience after Caesar has left. Discuss the effects of this soliloquy on your view of Caesar and Calpurnia.

Record your improvised scene in your logbook.

✺ Caesar beware!

Caesar has not listened to the warnings of the Soothsayer or his wife, but has been persuaded to go to the Capitol by the flattery of Decius and his ambition to be crowned king. One more warning is offered to Caesar, but he also resists this.

Work in groups of four. One of you should take on the role of Caesar, and the others take on the roles of Calpurnia, the Soothsayer and Artemidorus. Create a chorus scene in which Caesar stands in the centre and the three other characters speak the lines below. Experiment with intercutting or overlaying the lines so that you create an effect of voices of wisdom meeting the intransigence of the man.

CALPURNIA   Your wisdom is consumed in confidence.
                Do not go forth today. Call it my fear
                That keeps you in the house, and not your own.

SOOTHSAYER   Beware the Ides of March.
                The Ides of March are come: but not yet gone.

ARTEMIDORUS   Caesar, beware of Brutus, take heed of Cassius, come not
                near Casca, have an eye to Cinna, trust not Trebonius,
                mark well Metellus Cimber, Decius Brutus loves thee
                not, thou hast wronged Caius Ligarius. There is but one
                mind in all these men, and it is bent against Caesar. If
                thou beest not immortal look about you: security gives
                way to conspiracy. The mighty gods defend thee!

Write a description of these scenes in your logbook.

※ *Most puissant Caesar*

The murder of Caesar takes place in the Capitol in public so that it can be seen to be a worthy act rather than an act of revenge on the part of the conspirators. Caesar is seated on the throne and, as is customary, senators approach him with petitions. In the process, Popillius approaches Cassius and whispers to him. Cassius fears their conspiracy has been discovered.

It is the petition of Metellus Cimber to have his exiled brother returned to Rome that provides the opportunity for the murder of Caesar.

Work in a large group. Set up a series of depictions for each of the stages in the action of this scene outlined below. The stages have also been grouped into sections. You may wish to take each section at a time.

1 Caesar moves through the procession and makes his way to the throne.
2 The crowd hails Caesar.
3 Mark Antony places himself near Caesar.
4 Popillius approaches Cassius and whispers to him.
5 Brutus asks Cassius what Popillius has said.
6 Popillius approaches Caesar.
7 Brutus and Cassius watch him closely, but are relieved to see Caesar smile.

8 Trebonius draws Mark Antony into conversation away from Caesar.
9 Trebonius departs with Mark Antony.
10 Caesar holds up his hands for silence and addresses the throng of Senators.

11 Metellus Cimber moves forward and kneels before Caesar.
12 Caesar brushes him aside with a wave of the hand.
13 Metellus Cimber looks around to the senators for support.
14 Brutus comes forward and kisses Caesar's hand.
15 Cassius comes forward and kneels in front of Caesar.
16 Caesar refuses to be moved.
17 Decius kneels before Caesar.
18 Cinna comes close to Caesar.

19 Casca approaches Caesar with dagger drawn.
20 Casca stabs Caesar.
21 Cinna stabs Caesar.
22 Decius stabs Caesar.
23 Metellus Cimber stabs Caesar.
24 Cassius stabs Caesar.
25 Brutus stabs Caesar.
26 Caesar falls dead at the foot of the statue of Pompey.

27 Conspirators rejoice.
28 Brutus calms conspirators.

29 Brutus shepherds the older senators out of the senate.

30 Trebonius returns with the news that Antony has fled to his house.

31 The conspirators wash their hands in the spilt blood of Caesar.

When you have established these depictions you may wish to use some of the lines below to include in the depictions.

4 POPILLIUS   I wish your enterprise today may thrive.

5 BRUTUS   What said Popillius Lena?

   CASSIUS   He wished today our enterprise might thrive.
                 I fear our purpose is discoveréd.

7 BRUTUS   Cassius, be constant.
                 Popillius Lena speaks not of our purposes,
                 For look he smiles, and Caesar doth not change.

10 CAESAR   Are we all ready? What is now amiss
                 That Caesar and his Senate must redress?

11 METELLUS   Most high, most mighty, and most puissant Caesar,
                 Metellus Cimber throws before thy seat
                 An humble heart.

12 CAESAR   I must prevent thee, Cimber.
                 These couchings and these lowly courtesies
                 Might fire the blood of ordinary men.
                 Thy brother by decree is banishèd:
                 If thou dost bend, and pray, and fawn for him,
                 I spurn thee like a cur out of my way.

13 METELLUS   Is there no voice more worthy than my own
                 To sound more sweetly in great Caesar's ear?

14 BRUTUS   I kiss thy hand, but not in flattery, Caesar.

15 CASSIUS   Pardon, Caesar! Caesar, pardon!
                 As low as to thy foot doth Cassius fall.

16 CAESAR   I could be well moved, if I were as you;
                 If I could pray to move, prayers would move me.
                 But I am constant as the northern star,
                 Of whose true-fixed and resting quality
                 There is no fellow in the firmament.
                 Men are flesh and blood, and apprehensive;
                 Yet in the number I do know but one
                 That unassailable holds on his rank,
                 Unshaked of motion, and that I am he.

17 DECIUS   Great Caesar!

18	CINNA	O Caesar!

19	CASCA	Speak hands for me!

26	CAESAR	*Et tu, Brute?* – Then fall, Caesar!

27 CINNA Liberty! Freedom! Tyranny is dead!
Liberty, freedom and enfranchisement!

28 BRUTUS People and senators, be not affrighted,
Fly not, stand still! Ambition's debt is paid.

29 BRUTUS Let no man abide this deed
But we the doers.

30 TREBONIUS Antony is fled to his house amazed.

31 BRUTUS   Stoop, Romans, stoop,
And let us bathe our hands in Caesar's blood
Up to the elbows and besmear our swords.
Then walk we forth, even to the market-place,
And waving our red weapons o'er our heads
Let's all cry, 'Peace, freedom, and liberty!'

CASSIUS Stoop then and wash.

BRUTUS How many times shall Caesar bleed in sport,
That now on Pompey's basis lies along
No worthier than the dust!

CASSIUS   So oft as that shall be,
So often shall the knot of us be called
The men that gave their country liberty.

Discuss these depictions. Record the actions for each stage in your logbook as a storyboard script.

✶ *Or else were this a savage spectacle*

The focus of the next scene is on the bleeding body of Caesar and on the bloodied hands of the conspirators.

Set up a depiction in which the conspirators form a semicircle around the body of Caesar. Remember that the body lies at the foot of the statue of Pompey. Have each conspirator speak his feelings, aloud to the audience, about Caesar and the deed that he has participated in.

Show your depiction to other groups. Spend some time talking about the feelings that each conspirator has expressed.

Record a description of your depictions in your logbook.

❈ O mighty Caesar!

The conspirators, at Brutus' request, had agreed not to touch Mark Antony. After the deed, they have to deal with him and make decisions that will affect Mark Antony's ability to sway opinion against them.

Set up your depiction of the conspirators around the body of Caesar and add Mark Antony to the depiction. Where will he be positioned? Antony should speak last. You may wish to include his lines printed below.

ANTONY   O mighty Caesar! Dost thou lie so low?
       Are all thy conquests, glories, triumphs, spoils
       Shrunk to this little measure? Fare thee well!

Write a description of this scene in your logbook.

❈ Beg not your death of us

Mark Antony is a shrewd man who knows how to manipulate not only the conspirators but also the Roman people.

Set up the final moment of the previous depiction with Mark Antony's speech over Caesar. Improvise the next moment in this scene.

Spend time discussing your improvisations.

Read through the following edited version of the next moment of this scene. Use some of these lines in your improvisations.

ANTONY   I know not, gentlemen, what you intend,
       Who else must be let blood, who else is rank.
       If myself, there is no hour so fit
       As Caesar's death's hour, nor no instrument
       Of half that worth as those your swords made rich
       With the most noble blood of all this world.
       I do beseech ye, if you bear me hard,
       Now, whilst your purpled hands do reek and smoke,
       Fulfil your pleasure. Live a thousand years,
       I shall not find myself so apt to die.

BRUTUS   O Antony, beg not your death of us.
       Though now we must appear bloody and cruel,
       Our hearts you see are not, they are pitiful;
       And pity to the general wrong of Rome
       Hath done this deed on Caesar.

CASSIUS   Your voice shall be as strong as any man's
       In the disposing of new dignities.

BRUTUS   Only be patient till we have appeased
                           The multitude, beside themselves with fear,
                           And then we will deliver you the cause.

Record your improvisations in your logbook.

❊ *My credit now stands on such slippery ground*

The blood of Caesar is a powerful visual image. Its force is amplified in the next stage of the scene. Mark Antony shakes hands with the conspirators one by one, so that Caesar's blood, in which they have washed their hands, is visibly connecting all of them and drawing Mark Antony into their net. It is also an action which echoes the earlier scene with the binding of the conspirators.

Work in a group of eight. Set up a slow motion sculpture that shows Mark Antony shaking hands with each of the conspirators one by one:

- Brutus
- Cassius
- Decius
- Metellus Cimber
- Cinna
- Casca
- Trebonius.

Experiment with the way that he would shake hands with each one. You may wish to use theatrical blood to see the effect of the blooding of the conspirators. Show your slow motion sculpture to other groups and discuss the images in each.

Record your actions in your logbook.

❋ *Pardon me, Julius!*

Antony is constantly aware of the body of Caesar as he shakes hands with the conspirators. Set up the slow motion sculptures and freeze immediately after the shaking of hands with Trebonius. Allow Antony to speak this monologue over the body of Caesar.

ANTONY   That I did love thee, Caesar, O, 'tis true.
        If then thy spirit look upon us now,
        Shall it not grieve thee dearer than thy death
        To see thy Antony making his peace,
        Shaking the bloody fingers of thy foes?
        Had I as many eyes as thou hast wounds,
        Weeping as fast as they stream forth thy blood,
        It would become me better than to close
        In terms of friendship with thine enemies.
        Pardon me, Julius! Here wast thou bayed, brave hart,
        Here didst thou fall, and here thy hunters stand,
        Signed in thy spoil, and crimsoned in thy Lethe.
        O world! Thou wast the forest to this hart,
        And this indeed, O world, the heart of thee.
        How like a deer strucken by many princes
        Dost thou here lie!

Explore how the conspirators might react to this speech. Will someone interrupt or stop it, or will they let him go on? Discuss your improvisation with other groups.

Record these actions in your logbook.

❋ *What compact mean you to have with us?*

Antony manages to stitch the conspirators into the deal that will eventually lead to their overturn. Only Cassius expresses suspicions of his motives and his ability to sway the people.

Use some of the following lines to construct a scene that shows this reaction.

CASSIUS	Will you be pricked in number of our friends, Or shall we on and not depend on you?
ANTONY	Friends am I with you all, and love you all, Upon this hope, that you shall give me reasons Why and wherein Caesar was dangerous.
BRUTUS	Our reasons are so full of good regard You should be satisfied.
ANTONY	That's all I seek, And am, moreover, suitor that I may Produce his body to the market-place, And in the pulpit, as becomes a friend, Speak in the order of his funeral.
BRUTUS	You shall, Mark Antony. You shall not in your funeral speech blame us, But speak all good you can devise of Caesar And say you do't by our permission, Else shall you not have any hand at all About his funeral. And you shall speak In the same pulpit whereto I am going, After my speech is ended.
ANTONY	I do desire no more.

How do the conspirators depart? Are they all comfortable with Brutus' decision? How could you show this without using words?

Write your ideas in your logbook.

❋ *O pardon me, thou bleeding piece of earth*

Set up the final moment of your previous improvisation. Mark Antony is left on the stage as the conspirators depart. Does he watch them go? What is he feeling and thinking? What does he do? What does he say?

Printed below is an edited version of the monologue which Antony speaks over the body of Caesar. It is a precursor for the speech that will win him the good opinion and loyalty of the people at Caesar's funeral.

Work with a small group. Rehearse these lines.

ANTONY   O, pardon me, thou bleeding piece of earth,
That I am meek and gentle with these butchers!
Thou art the ruins of the noblest man
That ever livèd in the tide of times.
Woe to the hand that shed this costly blood!
Over thy wounds now do I prophesy
A curse shall light upon the limbs of men:
Domestic fury and fierce civil strife,
Blood and destruction shall be so in use
That mothers shall but smile when they behold
Their infants quartered with the hands of war,
And Caesar's spirit, ranging for revenge,
Shall in these confines with a monarch's voice
Cry havoc and let slip the dogs of war.

Why is this such a crucial speech?
Write your ideas in your logbook.

✷ *Friends, Romans, countrymen, and lovers*

Both Brutus and Mark Antony make public orations at the funeral of Caesar. Both attempt to move the crowd to their viewpoint. Both are successful. Brutus, however, makes the mistake of departing without hearing Antony's speech.

Edited versions of the two speeches are set out below. Work in a large group. Read through the speeches, then improvise a scene where Brutus makes his speech to the crowd. At the beginning the crowd is confused and angry and they do not understand the reasons for the actions of the conspirators. Encourage the crowd to listen carefully and to respond and interject to show how effectively Brutus is moving them to change their view of Caesar's death.

Repeat the improvisation with Antony's speech. Remember that at the beginning of this speech the crowd has accepted Brutus' explanation of Caesar's ambition and has been persuaded that the correct action has been taken by Brutus and the conspirators.

You may wish to consult chapter 1 for information about the prose and verse forms.

BRUTUS

Romans, countrymen, and lovers, hear me for my cause, and be silent that you may hear. Believe me for mine honour, and have respect to mine honour that you may believe. Censure me in your wisdom, and awake your senses that you may the better judge. If there be any in this assembly, any dear friend of Caesar's, to him I say that Brutus' love to Caesar was no less than his. If then that friend demand why Brutus rose against Caesar, this is my answer: not that I loved Caesar less, but that I loved Rome more. Had you rather Caesar were living, and die all slaves, than that Caesar were dead, to live all freeman? As Caesar loved me, I weep for him; as he was fortunate, I rejoice at it; as he was valiant, I honour him; but, as he was ambitious, I slew him. There is tears for his love, joy for his fortune, honour for his valour, and death for his ambition. Who is here so base that would be a bondman? If any, speak, for him have I offended. Who is here so rude that would not be a Roman? If any, speak, for him have I offended. Who is here so vile that will not love his country? If any, speak, for him have I offended. I have done no more to Caesar than you shall do to Brutus. The question of his death is enrolled in the Capitol, his glory not extenuated wherein he was worthy, nor his offences enforced for which he suffered death. As I slew my best lover for the good of Rome, I have the same dagger for myself when it shall please my country to need my death.

ANTONY

Friends, Romans, countrymen, lend me your ears!
I come to bury Caesar, not to praise him.
The evil that men do lives after them,
The good is oft interrèd with their bones:
So let it be with Caesar. The noble Brutus
Hath told you Caesar was ambitious;
If it were so, it was a grievous fault,
And grievously hath Caesar answered it.
Here, under leave of Brutus and the rest –
For Brutus is an honourable man,
So are they all, all honourable men –
Come I to speak in Caesar's funeral.
He was my friend, faithful and just to me,
But Brutus says he was ambitious,
And Brutus is an honourable man.
He hath brought many captives home to Rome,
Whose ransoms did the general coffers fill;

Did this in Caesar seem ambitious?
When that the poor hath cried, Caesar hath wept:
Ambition should be made of sterner stuff;
Yet Brutus says he was ambitious,
And Brutus is an honourable man.
You all did see that on the Lupercal
I thrice presented him a kingly crown,
Which he did thrice refuse. Was this ambition?
Yet Brutus says he was ambitious,
And sure he is an honourable man.
I speak not to disprove what Brutus spoke,
But here I am to speak what I do know.
You all did love him once, not without cause;
What cause withholds you then to mourn for him?
But yesterday the word of Caesar might
Have stood against the world; now lies he there,
And none so poor to do him reverence.
O masters, if I were disposed to stir
Your hearts and minds to mutiny and rage,
I should do Brutus wrong and Cassius wrong,
Who (you all know) are honourable men.
I will not do them wrong; I rather choose
To wrong the dead, to wrong myself and you,
Than I will wrong such honourable men.
It is not meet you know how Caesar loved you.
I have o'ershot myself to tell you of it
I fear I wrong the honourable men
Whose daggers have stabbed Caesar, I do fear it.
If you have tears, prepare to shed them now.
You all do know this mantle.
Look, in this place ran Cassius' dagger through;
See what a rent the envious Casca made;
Through this the well-belovèd Brutus stabbed;
And as he plucked his cursèd steel away,
Mark how the blood of Caesar followed it,
For Brutus, as you know, was Caesar's angel.
Judge, O you gods, how dearly Caesar loved him!
This was the most unkindest cut of all.
For when the noble Caesar saw him stab,
Ingratitude, more strong than traitor's arms,
Quite vanquished him. Then burst his mighty heart.
O, what a fall was there, my countrymen!
O, now you weep, and I perceive you feel
The dint of pity. These are gracious drops.

Kind souls, what weep you when you but behold
Our Caesar's vesture wounded? Look you here,
Here is himself, marred as you see, with traitors.
Good friends, sweet friends let me not stir you up
To such a sudden flood of mutiny.
They that have done this deed are honourable.
What private griefs they have, alas, I know not,
That made them do it. They are wise and honourable.
I come not, friends, to steal away your hearts.
For I have neither wit, nor words, nor worth,
Action, nor utterance, nor the power of speech
To stir men's blood. I only speak right on.
I tell you that which you yourselves do know,
Show you sweet Caesar's wounds, poor, poor, dumb mouths,
And bid them speak for me. But were I Brutus,
And Brutus Antony, there were an Antony
Would ruffle up your spirits and put a tongue
In every wound of Caesar, that should move
The stones of Rome to rise and mutiny.

❋ *Building the play*

You are now going to build your own play from these workshop explorations. Look back over the work that you have completed. Decide as a group which scenes could be incorporated in the playbuilt play. These could include:

- soundscape – Feast of Lupercal
- improvisation – Soothsayer
- monologue – Caesar
- tableau – processions
- duologue – Brutus and Cassius
- soliloquy – Cassius
- dumbshow – Casca
- images – storm
- scenes – conspirators
- soliloquy – Brutus
- dumbshow – conspirators
- split scene – Portia and Calpurnia
- scene – Caesar, Decius, Calpurnia
- chorus – beware

- depictions – murder
- scene – Mark Antony
- monologues – Mark Antony and Brutus.

Casting

You may wish to cast the roles for performance. Depending on the scenes you have chosen you will need to cast the roles of Caesar, Calpurnia, Brutus, Portia, Mark Antony, the conspirators, the Soothsayer, Roman citizens and any other characters you have created.

Linking the scenes

Consider what links are necessary between the scenes.

Rehearsing

You will need to revisit each scene and work on the staging and timing of each aspect.

Performing

When you have thoroughly rehearsed the play, present it to an audience and encourage the audience to give you feedback on their responses to the play.

You may wish to develop a printed program that provides your audience with information that you have explored throughout the playbuilding process.

Write your own responses to the play and the playbuilding process in your logbook. Keep a copy of the final script that you used for your performance.

When you have presented your version of the story, you may wish to explore the rest of Shakespeare's play, *Julius Caesar*.

Star-crossed Lovers

Romeo and Juliet

In this unit you are going to explore a story from one of Shakespeare's most famous plays, *Romeo and Juliet*. This story involves two feuding families and the eventual death of two young people as a direct result of the feuding. As you explore aspects of this story you will build up a play to perform. The play that you are going to build is set in a situation of constant tension between the two warring parties.

✳ *Preliminary discussion*

Work with a small group. Talk about the idea of feuds. What would make families or countries continue to fight over a number of generations? Think about some of the feuding situations that exist in the world today, e.g. Palestinians/Israelis, Serbs/Croats, Catholics/Protestants in Northern Ireland, Bosnia, Somalia, and so on.

Do some research about some of these. Try to find out what caused the friction in the first place and what keeps it going.

Write your ideas and information in your logbook.

✵ *I bite my thumb*

Work in small groups. Talk about insults that people hurl at one another.
Make a list of some of the words that are used as insults. Talk about gestures
that are used as insults. Many of these have sexual connotations. Research
how different cultures and different periods in history have used different
words or gestures as insults. In Elizabethan England, for instance, the gesture
of 'biting the thumb' was seen as a serious provocative insult. Experiment
with what this gesture might look like.

Record your explorations and discoveries in your logbook.

✵ *Do you quarrel, sir?*

Talk about how people react to insulting words and gestures. All too often
the reactions to an insulting remark or gesture can lead to further insults and
reactive gestures, and even to outbreaks of violence. Sometimes more and
more people become involved in the violence, taking sides according to
previous allegiances or in response to how they view the present situation.

Work in large groups. Set up a series of five freeze frames to demonstrate
a situation which begins with a single insulting gesture between two people.
In each successive frame add more and more people to show the escalation
of the violence.

When you have set up your frames, show them to other groups in the
class. Spend time talking about the ideas and issues that were raised in the
scene that results from the frames.

Replay the freeze frames, and this time think about the words that might
be said in each frame. Decide on who is speaking in each frame and explore
what is being said. Represent your frames to the other groups with these lines
being inserted.

Talk about how this affected the meanings and ideas of the frames. Record
these frames in your logbook as a storyboard script. Add the words as speech
balloons.

✵ *Enemies of peace*

Brawls are often ended by the intervention of a more powerful force, usually
someone with the status of an authority figure. Work in the same groups and
explore how the violent scene in the freeze frames could be stopped by the
intervention of an authority figure.

Set up two or three more frames that show how this occurs. You may need to adjust some of the earlier frames to free up a person to take the role of the authority figure.

Explore what the authority figure needs to say and do in order to stop the fracas.

Show your new frames to other groups in the class. Spend time discussing the issues being raised in this scene.

Record your new frames in your logbook as a storyboard script. Include the words as speech balloons.

✱ *Will they not hear?*

In the opening scene of *Romeo and Juliet* the Capulets and the Montagues engage in a fight such as the one you have constructed. This is eventually stopped by the Prince. Below you will find some of the words that the Prince speaks in order to stop the fight. Notice that at first, the fighting does not stop.

Work with a partner. Read through the speech. Experiment with the ways in which the Prince might say these lines.

PRINCE   Rebellious subjects, enemies of peace,
                Profaners of this neighbour-stainèd steel –
                Will they not hear? – What, ho, you men, you beasts!
                That quench the fire of your pernicious rage
                With purple fountains issuing from your veins:
                On pain of torture, from those bloody hands
                Throw your mistempered weapons to the ground,
                And hear the sentence of your movèd prince.
                If ever you disturb our streets again,
                Your lives shall pay the forfeit of the peace.
                For this time, all the rest depart away.
                Once more, on pain of death, all men depart.

Revisit your freeze frames. Try to incorporate the words and actions suggested by this speech into your freeze frames. You may need to adjust some aspects of your frames. You could try to use slow motion sculptures within each frame. Try to show how the men are reacting to the words that the Prince is saying as well as to each other.

Show your scenes to other groups in the class. Discuss the issues that these scenes raise. Record your ideas in your logbook.

✳ Who set this ancient quarrel new abroach?

The two warring families in this play are the Capulets and the Montagues. Romeo is a Montague and Juliet is a Capulet. Following the fight in the street the Prince has banned all public brawling and threatened to put to death anyone who disturbs the peace again.

Work in a small group. Talk about what effects that threat might have on the two sides. How would you feel about this if you were a Montague or a Capulet?

Imagine that you are either Capulets or Montagues. One of you should take on the role of the oldest of the clan – the head of the family. Improvise a scene where you discuss with the rest of the family the prohibition that the Prince has placed on public brawling.

Share your improvised scene with others in the class. Discuss the issues which these scenes have raised. Are there any solutions to the situation? What is the role of the head of the family in attempting to keep the violence under control?

Record the scene and write your ideas in your logbook.

✳ A man of wax

Work in groups of four. One member of your group should take on the role of a young girl, one should take on the role of the girl's alter ego and the others are the mother and the Nurse who has been nanny and companion to the girl all her life.

Improvise a scene where the two older women discuss the possibility of marriage and the benefits of it. Both older women will probably share a view of marriage that is quite foreign to the young girl. In the process of the discussion the mother tells the daughter that her father has picked out a young man as a potential husband for her.

In your improvisation, allow the girl's alter ego to comment to the audience on the things that the older women are saying and particularly the news of the potential husband.

Show your scene to the rest of the class. Discuss the issues raised by these scenes.

Write an outline of the script in your logbook.

❋ *If looking liking move*

Work with a partner. Imagine that the girl in the previous improvisation keeps a diary. Collaboratively write the entry she would make after this discussion about the potential husband. Explore ways in which the diary entry could be read in performance as the girl writes, either using speaking diary or voice-over.

❋ *I do love a woman*

Work with a partner. Both should take on the role of young men who are close friends. One is in love – unfortunately with a young woman in the opposing family. Improvise a scene in which the friends discuss this love affair.

How willing was the lover to talk about the woman? How helpful was the friend?

Now read the following section from the scene between Romeo and Benvolio, in which Romeo is revealing his love for Capulet's neice, Rosaline.

BENVOLIO   Tell me in sadness, who is that you love?

ROMEO   What, shall I groan and tell thee?

BENVOLIO   Groan? why, no;
But sadly tell me, who?

ROMEO   Bid a sick man in sadness make his will –
A word ill urged to one that is so ill:
In sadness, cousin, I do love a woman.

BENVOLIO   I aimed so near, when I supposed you loved.

ROMEO   A right good mark-man! and she's fair I love.

BENVOLIO   A right fair mark, fair coz, is soonest hit.

ROMEO   Well, in that hit you miss: she'll not be hit
With Cupid's arrow, she hath Dian's wit;
And in strong proof of chastity well armed,
From Love's weak childish bow she lives uncharmed.
She will not stay the siege of loving terms,
Nor bide th'encounter of assailing eyes,
Nor ope her lap to saint-seducing gold.
O, she is rich in beauty, only poor
That when she dies, with beauty dies her store.

BENVOLIO   Then she hath sworn that she will still live chaste?

ROMEO   She hath, and in that sparing makes huge waste;
For beauty starved with her severity

	Cuts beauty off from all posterity.
	She is too fair, too wise, wisely too fair,
	To merit bliss by making me despair.
	She hath forsworn to love, and in that vow
	Do I live dead, that live to tell it now.
BENVOLIO	Be ruled by me, forget to think of her.
ROMEO	O teach me how I should forget to think.
BENVOLIO	By giving liberty unto thine eyes,
	Examine other beauties.
ROMEO	'Tis the way

To call hers (exquisite) in question more:
These happy masks that kiss fair ladies' brows,
Being black, puts us in mind they hide the fair;
He that is strucken blind cannot forget
The precious treasure of his eyesight lost;
Show me a mistress that is passing fair,
What doth her beauty serve but as a note
Where I may read who passed that passing fair?
Farewell, thou canst not teach me to forget.

Rework your improvisation using some of these lines.
Record your ideas in your logbook.

❋ A fair assembly

Old Capulet decides that one way to deal with the situation of the ban on fighting and feuding is to have a ball for the Capulet family. This is a festive occasion in the midst of what has been some very unpleasant brawling. Capulet is trying to bond his entire family together with this celebratory activity. It is a masked fancy dress ball, so that it will not be easy to recognise faces behind the masks.

At this ball is the potential husband for Juliet, and the girl whom Romeo loves, Rosaline. The invitations to members of the Capulet family fall into the hands of the Montagues. Romeo, Mercutio and Benvolio also put on masks and attend the ball even though they are not Capulets.

Work in a large group. Design and make masks that these characters might wear to the ball. You may wish to research *commedia dell'arte* masks to assist you with your ideas.

Create a set of depictions, using the masks that you have made, to show aspects of the ball including the following:

- Capulet plays host
- Juliet's Nurse watches her

- Juliet's mother plays hostess
- Juliet's potential husband tries to impress her
- Juliet scrutinises the husband her father has chosen for her
- Romeo looks for Rosaline
- Benvolio and Mercutio watch Romeo
- guests dance
- guests dine
- musicians play
- servants pass around food and drinks
- and so on.

When you are satisfied with the depictions that you have constructed, arrange them in an order that tells the story of the ball. Experiment with sounds that could accompany each depiction, such as laughter, music and so on.

Present the depictions to an audience and seek a response from the members of the audience. Adjust or revise the depictions so that the story of the ball is clear to the audience.

Record these depictions and the sounds as a storyboard in your logbook.

⚹ Welcome, gentlemen!

Read through the following speech. It is the speech which Capulet makes as he welcomes the guests to the ball. Experiment with how he would say these lines. This speech could precede the set of depictions which you have created. Work out where all the guests are as the speech is made. Are the men on one side of the room and the ladies on the other? Look closely at the way Capulet goads the ladies who are pretending to be shy.

Replay the depictions, adding this speech at the beginning.

CAPULET   Welcome, gentlemen! Ladies that have their toes
                     Unplagued with corns will have a bout with you.
                     Ah, my mistresses, which of you all
                     Will now deny to dance? She that makes dainty,
                     She I'll swear hath corns. Am I come near ye now?
                     You are welcome, gentlemen. Come, musicians, play.
                     A hall, a hall, give room! and foot it, girls.

Spend some time discussing the issues that have been raised in this scene. Record your ideas in your logbook.

⚹ Fetch me my rapier

At the ball, Romeo sees Juliet for the first time. He is amazed at her beauty and asks a servant who she is. Tybalt, who is standing close by, recognises him as a Montague by his voice. Talk about how the voices of the Montagues and Capulets might differ.

Tybalt is enraged and wants to fight Romeo immediately, but Capulet intervenes and attempts to pacify him. Tybalt leaves the ball.

Create further depictions that show these aspects of the scenario.

You may wish to include some of the following lines in your depictions.

ROMEO	What lady's that which doth enrich the hand Of yonder knight?
TYBALT	This, by his voice, should be a Montague.
CAPULET	Why, how now, kinsman, wherefore storm you so?
TYBALT	Uncle, this is a Montague, our foe: A villain that is hither come in spite To scorn at our solemnity this night.
CAPULET	Content thee, gentle coz, let him alone, 'A bears him like a portly gentleman.
TYBALT	I'll not endure him.
CAPULET	Go to, go to, You are a saucy boy.

Talk about this scene. Was Capulet sensible to send Tybalt away? Record your ideas in your logbook.

✵ Come, musicians, play

After Tybalt leaves the ball, the two lovers meet for the first time in the process of the dance. You could research Elizabethan dancing to find out about the types of dances which were common at the time. You may also wish to research music from the period.

Work with a group to choreograph a dance that would allow Romeo and Juliet to be partners and unnoticed by others as they continue to dance. Record your ideas in your logbook.

✵ You kiss by th'book

Read through the lines which Shakespeare gives to the lovers as they dance. These speeches are in the form of sonnets, which were a common form of love poetry in the Elizabethan era. The two lovers speak one sonnet and begin a second one but do not finish this, as Juliet is called away by the Nurse.

ROMEO	If I profane with my unworthiest hand This holy shrine, the gentle sin is this, My lips, two blushing pilgrims, ready stand To smooth that rough touch with a tender kiss.
JULIET	Good pilgrim, you do wrong your hand too much, Which mannerly devotion shows in this,

	For saints have hands that pilgrims' hands do touch, And palm to palm is holy palmers' kiss.
ROMEO	Have not saints lips, and holy palmers too?
JULIET	Ay, pilgrim, lips that they must use in prayer.
ROMEO	O then, dear saint, let lips do what hands do: They pray, grant thou, lest faith turn to despair.
JULIET	Saints do move, though grant for prayers' sake.
ROMEO	Then move not, while my prayer's effect I take. Thus from my lips, by thine, my sin is purged.
JULIET	Then have my lips the sin that they have took.
ROMEO	Sin from my lips? O trespass sweetly urged! Give me my sin again.
JULIET	You kiss by th'book.

Explore ways in which these lines could be incorporated in the dance sequence which you have derived. Notice that Romeo kisses Juliet. You may wish to explore how this occurs. Think about Juliet's final comment. Is she complimenting Romeo or not?

Show your version of the lovers' sonnet meeting to others in the class. Spend some time discussing how this works on the stage.

Record your discoveries in your logbook.

✳ Now Romeo is beloved and loves again

Work in a group. Look back over the series of depictions which you have created for the ball scene. In some of these there is no movement and only sounds, while in others there is not only movement but also speech. Explore where you could insert the moments with Tybalt and with Romeo and Juliet. You may need to make some adaptations to the depictions.

When you have slotted these scenes in, rehearse the entire sequence and present it to an audience.

Record your ideas in your logbook.

✳ Madman! passion! lover!

Romeo has been smitten by love, and is doubly distressed to find himself so much in love with a Capulet – a love that makes life dangerous. His companions ridicule him.

Work in groups of three. Create a statue sculpture of Romeo showing his state of being in love. Place this frozen statue on one part of the performance space. In another part of the performance space improvise a scene between Mercutio and Benvolio after the ball. These two friends discuss Romeo's affliction. End the improvisation with the two friends leaving. Have the statue of Romeo turn to the audience and speak a soliloquy expressing his feelings. You may wish to consult chapter 1 for further information about soliloquy.

Show this scene to others in the class. Spend some time discussing the effects that it has on the audience.

Record the scene in your logbook.

✳ *Wherefore art thou Romeo?*

One of the most famous scenes in all of Shakespeare's plays is the balcony scene where Romeo and Juliet meet for the first time after the ball. Juliet is just as concerned about falling in love with a Montague as Romeo is at loving a Capulet. Juliet is on the balcony and Romeo is down below. Romeo overhears her confessions of love.

Explore how to make this scene work in performance. Where does Juliet need to be on the stage? Where could Romeo be on the stage? You may wish to research the stage at the Globe to explore how this scene would have worked on Shakespeare's stage.

Below you will find an edited version of this scene. Work with a partner and rehearse this scene. Explore ways in which to speak the verse. Remember that initially both are speaking directly to the audience, then they speak to each other.

ROMEO   It is my lady, O it is my love:
                       O that she knew she were!
                       She speaks, yet she says nothing; what of that?
                       I am too bold, 'tis not to me she speaks.
                       See, how she leans her cheek upon her hand!
                       O, that I were a glove upon that hand,
                       That I might touch that cheek!
                       O, speak again, bright angel, for thou art
                       As glorious to this night, being o'er my head,
                       As is a wingèd messenger of heaven.

JULIET   O Romeo, Romeo, wherefore art thou Romeo?
                       Deny thy father and refuse thy name;
                       Or if thou wilt not, be but sworn my love,
                       And I'll no longer be a Capulet.

What's in a name? That which we call a rose
By any other word would smell as sweet.
          Romeo, doff thy name,
And for thy name which is no part of thee,
Take all myself.

ROMEO   I take thee at thy word:
Call me but love, and I'll be new baptised;
Henceforth I never will be Romeo.

JULIET   What man art thou that thus bescreened in night
So stumblest on my counsel?

ROMEO   By a name
I know not how to tell thee who I am.

JULIET   My ears have yet not drunk a hundred words
Of that tongue's uttering, yet I know the sound.
Art thou not Romeo, and a Montague?

ROMEO   Neither, fair maid, if either thee dislike.

JULIET   How cam'st thou hither, tell me, and wherefore?

ROMEO   With love's light wings did I o'erperch these walls.

JULIET   By whose direction found'st thou out this place?

ROMEO   By Love, that first did prompt me to enquire.

JULIET   Dost thou love me? O gentle Romeo,
If thou dost love, pronounce it faithfully.
Or if thou think'st I am too quickly won,
I'll frown and be perverse, and say thee nay.
I should have been more strange, I must confess,
But that thou overheard'st, ere I was ware,
My true-love passion; therefore pardon me.

ROMEO   Lady, by yonder blessèd moon I vow.

JULIET   O swear not by the moon, th'inconstant moon.

ROMEO   What shall I swear by?

JULIET   Do not swear at all.
I have no joy of this contract tonight,
It is too rash, too unadvised, too sudden.
Good night, good night! as sweet repose and rest
Come to thy heart as that within my breast!

ROMEO   O, wilt thou leave me so unsatisfied?

JULIET   What satisfaction canst thou have tonight?

ROMEO   Th'exchange of thy love's faithful vow for mine.

JULIET   I gave thee mine before thou didst request it.

ROMEO	Wouldst thou withdraw it? for what purpose, love?
JULIET	But to be frank and give it thee again. I hear some noise within; dear love adieu!
ROMEO	O blessèd, blessèd night!

Record your explorations and discoveries in your logbook.

✳ *Parting is such sweet sorrow*

The scene ends with both lovers finding it difficult to go. Juliet goes indoors and returns. Romeo tries to drag himself away and is pulled back. Talk about how each of these characters might be feeling at this point.

With a partner, work out a movement sequence that shows the two lovers parting. You may wish to find some music to help you choreograph the sequence.

Show your version to the rest of the class. Spend some time discussing the ideas that this moment communicates. You may wish to go back to your version of the previous scene and incorporate this movement sequence in that scene.

Record your investigations and discoveries in your logbook.

✳ *To breathe such vows as lovers use to swear*

Romeo and Juliet are married by Friar Lawrence in his cell. It is a simple ceremony but obviously not the kind of marriage ceremony that Juliet's parents would have had in mind for her.

Work in groups of three. Improvise the marriage scene with the arrival of Romeo and then of Juliet. You may wish to incorporate some of the lines below. You will also need to consider the symbols that are usually associated with weddings. What symbols will you need for this scene?

FRIAR LAWRENCE	So smile the heavens upon this holy act, That after-hours with sorrow chide us not.
ROMEO	Amen, amen! but come what sorrow can, It cannot countervail the exchange of joy That one short minute gives me in her sight.
JULIET	But my true love is grown to such excess I cannot sum up sum of half my wealth.

Present your scene to the rest of the class. Encourage audience response.

Write the script of your scene in your logbook, including the details of movement and staging.

✵ *Alla stoccata*

The action which marks the turning point of the play is the death of Tybalt. This takes place in a fight scene in the street. In one sense it is a repetition of the opening brawl scene, but this time the Prince does not get there before Mercutio is wounded by Tybalt, Romeo is drawn into the fight, Tybalt is killed by Romeo and Romeo has fled.

Work with a large group. Choreograph a slow motion sculpture of this fight scene. The stages in the scene are listed below.

• Benvolio and Mercutio enter in a quarrelsome mood
• Tybalt and others enter and provoke them
• Romeo enters and Tybalt challenges him
• Romeo tries to calm him down
• Benvolio draws his sword and attacks
• Tybalt responds
• Romeo tries to stop the fight
• Mercutio is wounded
• Tybalt and his friends flee
• Romeo organises people to carry Mercutio to a doctor
• Benvolio comes back with the news of Mercutio's death
• Tybalt comes back still furious
• Romeo attacks him in revenge for Mercutio's death
• Romeo kills Tybalt
• Romeo flees
• the citizens enter with the Prince
• Lady Capulet is distraught
• the Capulets and Montagues both demand justice
• the Prince announces Romeo's banishment.

You may wish to use some of the lines of the Prince in the final moment.

PRINCE   I will be deaf to pleading and excuses.
            Romeo slew [Tybalt], he slew Mercutio;
            Who now the price of his dear blood doth owe?
                          And for that offence
            Immediately we do exile him hence.
                          Let Romeo hence in haste,
            Else, when he's found, that hour is his last.

Show your slow motion sculptures to the rest of the class. Discuss the effects of this portrayal of the fight and Romeo's banishment.

Record your investigations in your logbook.

✳ *Gallop apace*

Juliet waits impatiently for Romeo to come to her bedroom on the night of her wedding. Her impatience grows until the Nurse arrives with the news of Tybalt's death and Romeo's banishment.

Work with a partner. Read through the following lines. They are taken from the monologue which Juliet speaks as she is waiting for Romeo. Experiment with voice, gesture and movement that Juliet might use as she speaks the lines.

Gallop apace, you fiery-footed steeds.

Spread thy close curtain, love-performing Night.

Leap to these arms, untalked of and unseen.

Come, civil Night,
Thou sober-suited matron all in black,
And learn me how to lose a winning match,
Played for a pair of stainless maidenhoods:

Come, Night, come, Romeo, come, thou day in night;

Come, gentle Night, come, loving, black-browed Night,
Give me my Romeo.

O, I have bought the mansion of a love,
But not possessed it, and though I am sold,
Not yet enjoyed.

Work with your partner. One of you should take on the role of Juliet and the other should take on the role of the Nurse. Improvise a monologue in which Juliet tells the audience about her longing for Romeo and the night that they may have together. You may wish to use some of the words from the lines you have read.

When Juliet is in the heights of expectation, the Nurse should enter the scene obviously distraught but without telling Juliet what has happened. Juliet can see that something is wrong but she must find out about the events in the street by asking questions.

When the whole story has been told, discuss how Juliet feels about the situation of Romeo's banishment. Compare her mood before and after the news.

Record your improvisation in your logbook.

✵ 'Tis torture, and not mercy

At the same moment that Juliet is comforted by the Nurse, Romeo is also being counselled by the Friar. While Juliet has been waiting for the Nurse to return, Romeo has also been waiting for the Friar who has been to see the Prince. The judgement which he brings with him is 'banishment'. For Romeo that is as bad as death. Romeo begins to rave and the Friar makes many attempts to interrupt but without a great deal of success.

Below is one of Romeo's speeches from this scene. Work with a partner. Read this speech. Discuss the tone of voice that could be used to communicate the feeling of these lines.

ROMEO   'Tis torture, and not mercy. Heaven is here
                           Where Juliet lives, and every cat and dog
                           And little mouse, every unworthy thing,
                           Live here in heaven, and may look on her,
                           But Romeo may not. More validity,
                           More honourable state, more courtship lives
                           In carrion flies than Romeo; they may seize
                           On the white wonder of dear Juliet's hand,
                           And steal immortal blessing from her lips,
                           Who even in pure and vestal modesty
                           Still blush, as thinking their own kisses sin;
                           But Romeo may not; he is banishèd.
                           Flies may do this, but I from this must fly;
                           They are free men, but I am banishèd:
                           And sayest thou yet that exile is not death?
                           Hadst thou no poison mixed, no sharp-ground knife,
                           No sudden mean of death, though ne'er so mean,
                           But 'banishèd' to kill me? 'Banishèd'?
                           O Friar, the damnèd used that word in hell;
                           Howling attends it. How hast thou the heart,
                           Being a divine, a ghostly confessor,
                           A sin-absolver, and my friend professed,
                           To mangle me with that word 'banishèd'?

Work with a partner. One of you should take on the role of Romeo and the other of the Friar. Improvise a scene in which Romeo raves about the pain of his banishment and the Friar attempts to counsel him. You may wish to incorporate some of the words or lines from the speech you have read.

Record your improvisation in your logbook.

Set up a scene using a split stage with Romeo and the Friar on one side and Juliet and the Nurse on the other side. Intercut the segments of the two scenes that you have just improvised. What effects does this have on the view of Romeo and Juliet?

Record your ideas in your logbook.

Hie to your chamber

The Nurse had brought with her some 'cords'. This was a kind of rope ladder which Romeo was to use to climb in to Juliet's bedroom that night. Sketch what these 'cords' might look like.

At the end of the scene where Juliet learns of the deaths of Tybalt and Mercutio and Romeo's banishment, she focuses on these cords. Read the segment of text below. Rehearse this moment with a partner.

JULIET   Take up those cords. Poor ropes, you are beguiled,
        Both you and I, for Romeo is exiled.
        He made you for a highway to my bed,
        But I, a maid, die maiden-widowèd.
        Come, cords, come, Nurse, I'll to my wedding bed,
        And death, not Romeo, take my maidenhead!

NURSE   Hie to your chamber. I'll find Romeo
        To comfort you, I wot well where he is.
        Hark ye, your Romeo will be here at night.

JULIET   O find him! Give this ring to my true knight,
        And bid him come to take his last farewell.

Record your explorations in your logbook.

Hold thy desperate hand

Just as the Nurse takes control of Juliet, so does the Friar eventually take control of Romeo, just as he draws his sword with the intention of taking his own life.

Below is an edited version of the speech which the Friar finally makes to calm Romeo and help him to take control of his actions. Work with a partner. Rehearse this moment. Explore how the two characters interact as the Friar gives 'the lecture' to Romeo.

FRIAR LAWRENCE   Hold thy desperate hand!
      Art thou a man? thy form cries out thou art;
      Thy tears are womanish, thy wild acts denote
      The unreasonable fury of a beast.
      Thou hast amazed me. By my holy order,
      I thought thy disposition better tempered.
      Hast thou slain Tybalt? wilt thou slay thyself,
      And slay thy lady that in thy life lives,
      By doing damnèd hate upon thyself?
      Fie, fie, thou sham'st thy shape, thy love, thy wit,
      Thy noble shape is but a form of wax,

	Digressing from the valour of a man;
	Thy dear love sworn but hollow perjury,
	Killing that love which thou hast vowed to cherish;
	What, rouse thee, man! thy Juliet is alive,
	For whose dear sake thou wast but lately dead:
	Happiness courts thee in his best array,
	But like a misbehavèd and sullen wench,
	Thou pouts upon thy fortune and thy love:
	Take heed, take heed, for such die miserable.
	Go get thee to thy love as was decreed,
	Ascend her chamber, hence and comfort her;
	But look thou stay not till the Watch be set,
	For then thou canst not pass to Mantua,
	Where thou shalt live till we can find a time
	To blaze your marriage, reconcile your friends,
	Beg pardon of the Prince, and call thee back
	With twenty hundred thousand times more joy
	Than thou went'st forth in lamentation.

ROMEO   But that a joy past joy calls out on me,
          It were a grief, so brief to part with thee.

Record your ideas in your logbook.

❋ *More light and light*

The consummation of their love leads to the agony of parting. Work with a partner and read through the following speeches, then improvise a scene based on these speeches. You may wish to use some of the lines from these speeches in your improvisations.

JULIET   Wilt thou be gone? It is not yet near day:
          It was the nightingale, and not the lark,
          That pierced the fearful hollow of thine ear;
          Nightly she sings on yond pomegranate tree.
          Believe me, love, it was the nightingale.

ROMEO   It was the lark, the herald of the morn,
          No nightingale. Look, love, what envious streaks
          Do lace the severing clouds in yonder east:
          Night's candles are burnt out, and jocund day
          Stands tiptoe on the misty mountain tops.
          I must be gone and live, or stay and die.

JULIET   Yond light is not daylight, I know it, I:
          It is some meteor that the sun exhaled,

To be to thee this night a torch-bearer,
And light thee on thy way to Mantua.
Therefore stay yet, thou need'st not to be gone.

ROMEO   Let me be tane, let me be put to death,
I am content, so thou wilt have it so.
I'll say yon grey is not the morning's eye,
'Tis but the pale reflex of Cynthia's brow;
Nor that is not the lark whose notes do beat
The vaulty heaven so high above our heads.
I have more care to stay than will to go:
Come, death, and welcome! Juliet wills it so.
How is't, my soul? Let's talk, it is not day.

JULIET   It is, it is, hie hence, be gone, away!
It is the lark that sings so out of tune,
Straining harsh discords and unpleasing sharps.
Some say the lark makes sweet division:
This doth not so, for she divideth us.
Some say the lark and loathèd toad changed eyes;
O now I would they had changed voices too,
Since arm from arm that voice doth us affray,
Hunting thee hence with hunt's-up to the day.
O now be gone, more light and light it grows.

ROMEO   More light and light, more dark and dark our woes!
Farewell, farewell! one kiss, and I'll descend.

JULIET   Art thou gone so, love, lord, ay husband, friend?
I must hear from thee every day in the hour,
For in a minute there are many days.
O, by this count I shall be much in years
Ere I again behold my Romeo!

ROMEO   Farewell!
I will omit no opportunity
That may convey my greetings, love, to thee.

JULIET   O think'st thou we shall ever meet again?

ROMEO   I doubt it not, and all these woes shall serve
For sweet discourses in our times to come.

JULIET   O God, I have an ill-divining soul!
Methinks I see thee now, thou art so low,
As one dead in the bottom of a tomb.
Either my eyesight fails, or thou look'st pale.

ROMEO   And trust me, love, in my eye so do you:
Dry sorrow drinks our blood. Adieu, adieu!

Record your improvisation and your ideas in your logbook.

So worthy a gentleman to be her bride

Juliet is, of course, distraught at the departure of Romeo, but this is by no means the end of her woes. Her parents have decided that the distress of the loss of Tybalt, her cousin, and the family disruptions can best be healed by the marriage of Juliet to Paris.

Work in groups of three. One of you should take on the role of Juliet and the others should take on the roles of Juliet's mother and father. Improvise a scene where the parents try to persuade Juliet to stop the weeping, which they think is for the death of Tybalt, and prepare herself for marriage to Paris. In this improvisation Juliet is to speak only the following lines – to her father:

> Good father, I beseech you on my knees,
> Hear me with patience but to speak a word.

– and to her mother:

> O sweet my mother, cast me not away!

Juliet will probably need to speak these lines several times as the parents become more and more angry with her unwillingness to agree to the marriage.

End the improvisation with the following lines:

FATHER   For by my soul, I'll ne'er acknowledge thee.

MOTHER   Talk not to me, for I'll not speak a word.

Discuss how Juliet feels to be so rejected by her parents. Record your ideas in your logbook.

Take thou this vial

The action of the rest of the play depends upon the poisons which both Juliet and Romeo use. Juliet's poison simply simulates death while Romeo's ensures death. Think about the vial that holds this poison. Look for two bottles that could be used as props in the play.

Record your ideas in your logbook.

✖ *Pardon, I beseech you!*

Once Juliet has the vial of poison and the plan laid out by Friar Lawrence, she is able to play a duplicitous game with her parents.

Work in groups of three. One of you should take on the role of Juliet and the others should take on the roles of the parents. Create a depiction with Juliet kneeling to her parents in apparent obedience. Show the parents' responses to her changed attitude. Think about where the vial of poison is. Can the audience see this? Can her parents see this?

When you are satisfied with your depiction, have each of the characters speak a short monologue to the audience. The other characters remain in a freeze, indicating to the audience that they have not heard the inner thoughts of the other characters.

Record your ideas in your logbook.

�֍ *Come vial*

Juliet approaches the drinking of the poison with due fear and apprehension.

Below you will find the monologue from the play which she speaks before she drinks the poison. She has both the poison and a dagger with her as she speaks. Work in a group. The speech is broken into sections to help you trace the stages in her argument and the moods she goes through. Read through the speech together.

JULIET   My dismal scene I needs must act alone.

I have a faint cold fear thrills through my veins
That almost freezes up the heat of life:
Come, vial.

What if this mixture do not work at all?
Shall I be married then tomorrow morning?
No, no, this shall forbid it; lie thou there.

What if it be a poison which the Friar
Subtly hath ministered to have me dead,
Lest in this marriage he should be dishonoured,
Because he married me before to Romeo?

I fear it is, and yet methinks it should not,
For he hath still been tried a holy man.

How if, when I am laid into the tomb,
I wake before the time that Romeo
Come to redeem me? There's a fearful point!

Shall I not then be stifled in the vault,
To whose foul mouth no healthsome air breathes in,
And there die strangled ere my Romeo comes?

Or if I live, is it not very like
The horrible conceit of death and night,
Together with the terror of the place –

As in a vault, an ancient receptacle,
Where for this many hundred years the bones
Of all my buried ancestors are packed,
Where bloody Tybalt, yet but green in earth,
Lies fest'ring in his shroud, where, as they say,
At some hours in the night spirits resort –

Alack, alack, is it not like that I,
So early waking – what with loathsome smells,
And shrieks like mandrakes' torn out of the earth,
That living mortals hearing them run mad –

O, if I wake, shall I not be distraught,
Environèd with all these hideous fears,
And madly play with my forefathers' joints,
And pluck the mangled Tybalt from his shroud,
And in this rage, with some great kinsman's bone,
As with a club, dash out my desp'rate brains?

O look! methinks I see my cousin's ghost
Seeking out Romeo that spit his body
Upon a rapier's point. Stay, Tybalt, stay!

Romeo, Romeo, Romeo! Here's drink – I drink to thee.

One of you should take on the role of Juliet. In this scene Juliet will speak only the first and last lines of this monologue.

The other members of the group should become a chorus. Each member of the chorus should take a section of the speech except for the first and last lines. Rehearse your section of the speech, looking for key words that indicate how Juliet is feeling.

Juliet should take up a position in the centre of the space. She is holding the vial and the dagger. Throughout the scene Juliet responds to the chorus of voices by echoing the key words that reveal her feelings as the chorus speaks the lines around her.

The chorus should be arranged around Juliet. As you speak the lines to Juliet she will echo some of the words and respond by showing how she is feeling. The scene ends with Juliet drinking the poison.

Record this scene in your logbook.

✻ You slug-a-bed

The discovery of Juliet by the Nurse is in stark contrast to the previous scene. Work in groups of six. Set up a series of freeze frames that show the discovery of Juliet's supposedly dead body. The frames should show:

- Juliet lying 'dead'
- the Nurse finding her
- the arrival of the mother
- the arrival of the father
- the arrival of Paris, her would-be husband
- the arrival of Friar Lawrence.

Try to show the different reactions of the characters to the apparent death of Juliet.

Replay the freeze frames, with each character, except Juliet, speaking a line as they come face to face with the sight.

Record your ideas in your logbook.

�֎ *Most woeful day!*

Work in groups of six. Read through the section of this scene printed below. In this section, each of the characters speaks a short monologue. It is almost as if each one is speaking to the audience rather than to each other.

LADY CAPULET	Accursed, unhappy, wretched, hateful day!
	Most miserable hour that e'er time saw
	In lasting labour of his pilgrimage!
	But one, poor one, one poor and loving child,
	But one thing to rejoice and solace in,
	And cruel Death hath catched it from my sight!
NURSE	O woe! O woeful, woeful, woeful day!
	Most lamentable day, most woeful day
	That ever, ever, I did yet behold!
	O day, O day, O day, O hateful day!
	Never was seen so black a day as this.
	O woeful day, O woeful day!
PARIS	Beguiled, divorcèd, wronged, spited, slain!
	Most detestable Death, by thee beguiled,
	By cruel, cruel thee quite overthrown!
	O love! O life! not life, but love in death!
CAPULET	Despised, distressèd, hated, martyred, killed!
	Uncomfortable time, why cam'st thou now
	To murder, murder our solemnity?
	O child, O child! my soul, and not my child!
	Dead art thou. Alack, my child is dead,
	And with my child my joys are buried.
FRIAR LAWRENCE	Peace ho, for shame! Confusion's cure lives not
	In these confusions. Heaven and yourself

Had part in this fair maid, now heaven hath all,
And all the better is it for the maid:
Your part in her you could not keep from death,
But heaven keeps his part in eternal life.
The most you sought was her promotion,
For 'twas your heaven she should be advanced,
And weep ye now, seeing she is advanced
Above the clouds, as high as heaven itself?
O, in this love, you love your child so ill
That you run mad, seeing that she is well.
She's not well married that lives married long,
But she's best married that dies married young.
Dry up your tears, and stick your rosemary
On this fair corse, and as the custom is,
And in her best array, bear her to church;
For though fond nature bids us all lament,
Yet nature's tears are reason's merriment.

Each member of the group should take one of the speeches and rehearse it as a monologue, then replay the freeze frames from the previous activity and insert these speeches into each frame. Show these to an audience and seek a response.

Record your ideas in your logbook.

✴ *Follow this fair corse to her grave*

Research music that is used in funerals. There are several requiems that express the sorrow and sadness of the loss of a loved one. Select a section of one of these pieces of music, or alternatively devise your own music for a funeral march.

Work in groups. Begin with the final moment of the previous set of freeze frames. Juliet is lying on her bed, dead. The five characters have each reacted to the scene. Now, at the admonition of the Friar, the body of Juliet is to be lifted and carried in a funeral procession. You will need to rehearse the lift carefully.

Experiment with different ways of lifting and carrying the body of Juliet. Explore how the characters show their feelings by the way they lift the body and begin to walk. Experiment with the roles that the two women play in this scene. Do they lift the body or watch the men do it?

Work out where the tomb could be on the stage. Is this a raised area? Rehearse the scene from the discovery through to the placing of the body in the tomb.

Record your scenes in your logbook.

✴ *News from Verona*

In many of Shakespeare's plays the characters on stage, and the audience, receive news from messengers. At this point in *Romeo and Juliet*, Romeo receives the news of Juliet's death, but it is not unfortunately the news that Friar Lawrence had intended him to hear. The messenger carrying that news has been detained.

Work with a partner. Read the following segment from this duologue.

ROMEO
News from Verona! How now, Balthasar?
How doth my lady?
How doth my Juliet?
For nothing can be ill if she be well.

BALTHASAR
Then she is well and nothing can be ill:
Her body sleeps in Capel's monument,
And her immortal part with angels lives.
I saw her laid low in her kindred's vault.
O pardon me for bringing these ill news.

ROMEO
Is it e'en so? then I defy you, stars!
Thou knowest my lodging, get me ink and paper,
And hire post-horses; I will hence tonight.

BALTHASAR
I do beseech you, sir, have patience:
Your looks are pale and wild, and do import
Some misadventure.

ROMEO   Tush thou art deceived.
                     Leave me, and do the thing I bid thee do.

Rehearse these lines with your partner. How do the two characters interact?

Record your ideas in your logbook.

Well, Juliet, I will lie with thee tonight

The finale of this story of 'star-crossed lovers' brings everyone together at the Capulet tomb. This is a family vault which contains the bodies of members of the family who have died. Most recently, the bodies of Tybalt and Juliet have been added to this tomb.

Work in a small group. Your task is to design a stage set that will capture the mood of the scene for your audience. You may wish to research what monuments looked like and then explore how this could be communicated on a stage. Remember that you will need to make provision for the bodies of Tybalt and Juliet. In this scene there is further bloodshed, as Romeo kills Paris and brings his body into the tomb, and then Romeo himself dies. You will need to consider where these bodies will be placed within the set you design. Remember too, that anything too complex which has to be assembled between the scenes will interrupt the flow of the action. You will also need to explore the colours and textures which could communicate the mood of the scene.

When you have completed your sketches of the set for this scene, share them with other groups and discuss how the design that you have created could be constructed. Talk about the mood that will be conveyed to the audience.

Record your ideas in your logbook.

Thou womb of death

Work in a large group. Mark out in the playing space the set that you designed for this last scene. Identify where Tybalt's body is placed.

There is a number of people in this scene, most of whom have been in earlier scenes. Work in your group to sketch the costumes that they might be wearing at this point in the play. Remember that it is night, and some of these people have been called from their beds.

The characters in this scene include:

- Paris
- Page
- Romeo
- Balthasar
- Juliet
- Friar Lawrence
- guards
- Capulets
- Montagues
- Prince.

Spend some time discussing the issues that arise from this activity and record your ideas in your logbook.

✵ *Not so long as is a tedious tale*

The action of this scene moves quite swiftly to its inevitable doom. Work in a large group. Create a series of freeze frames for the steps in the action of this scene outlined below. You may wish to work with each section separately and then put the entire sequence together when you have constructed each of the sections.

1 Paris and Page arrive at the entrance to the tomb.
2 Page is pushed away by Paris.
3 Paris weeps and places flowers at the entrance.
4 Page warns him that someone is coming.
5 They hide.

6 Romeo and Balthasar arrive at the entrance to the tomb.
7 Romeo pushes Balthasar away.
8 Romeo opens the tomb.
9 Paris steps forward and challenges Romeo.
10 They fight.
11 Romeo kills Paris and Page runs away.

12 Balthasar watches Romeo.
13 Romeo carries Paris into the tomb and lays his body on a vault.
14 Romeo finds Juliet.
15 Romeo finds Tybalt.
16 Romeo lies beside Juliet.
17 Romeo kisses Juliet.
18 Romeo drinks the poison.

19 Romeo kisses Juliet again and dies.

20 Friar Lawrence arrives and is greeted by Balthasar.

21 Friar Lawrence sees Paris and Romeo.

22 Juliet wakes.

23 Friar tries to persuade her to leave.

24 Juliet sends Friar Lawrence away.

25 Juliet sees the cup that held the poison which Romeo has swallowed.

26 Juliet tries to drink the dregs of poison from the cup.

27 Juliet kisses Romeo.

28 Juliet takes his dagger and stabs herself.

29 Page returns with the guards, Juliet's parents, Romeo's parents, and the Prince.

30 They all survey the carnage as Friar Lawrence recounts what has happened and the Prince closes the events.

Use the technique of freeze-dissolve-freeze to connect these frames so that the action is continuous, but in slow motion. You may wish to explore the use of sound and silence to communicate the mood and meaning of each moment in the scene.

When you have set these freeze frames in place and connected them with a dissolve or slow motion sculpture technique, show them to another group or an audience from outside the class. Allow time for their responses and make any changes you think will help communicate the action and the mood.

Record your ideas in your logbook.

✖ *Death is amorous*

Revisit the moments in your freeze frames where Romeo (16–19) and Juliet (25–28) die. Romeo has a long monologue in the play at the point where he dies. Part of it is printed below. Juliet's monologue is much shorter, and her death more violent by contrast with Romeo's. Her monologue is also printed below.

Read through these lines and experiment with incorporating them into your frames.

ROMEO

> Ah, dear Juliet,
> Why art thou yet so fair? Shall I believe
> That unsubstantial Death is amorous,
> And that the lean abhorrèd monster keeps
> Thee here in dark to be his paramour?
> For fear of that, I will stay with thee,
> And never from this palace of dim night
> Depart again. Here, here will I remain
> With worms that are thy chambermaids; O here
> Will I set up my everlasting rest,
> And shake the yoke of inauspicious stars

From this world-wearied flesh. Eyes, look your last!
Arms, take your last embrace! and, lips, O you
The doors of breath, seal with a righteous kiss
A dateless bargain to engrossing Death!
Come, bitter conduct, come, unsavoury guide!
Thou desperate pilot, now at one run on
The dashing rocks thy seasick weary bark!
Here's to my love! O true apothecary!
Thy drugs are quick. Thus with a kiss I die.

JULIET   What's here? a cup closed in my true love's hand?
Poison I see hath been his timeless end.
O churl, drunk all, and left no friendly drop
To help me after? I will kiss thy lips,
Haply some poison yet doth hang on them,
To make me die with a restorative.
Thy lips are warm.
O happy dagger,
This is thy sheath; there rust, and let me die.

Record your ideas in your logbook.

❋ *Till we can clear these ambiguities*

Read through the Friar's explanation of the events printed below, and the
Prince's summing up of the situation. You may wish to incorporate some
aspects of these in your freeze frames.

FRIAR LAWRENCE   Romeo, there dead, was husband to that Juliet,
And she, there dead, that Romeo's faithful wife:
I married them, and their stol'n marriage day
Was Tybalt's doomsday, whose untimely death
Banished the new-made bridegroom from this city,
For whom, and not for Tybalt, Juliet pined.
You, to remove that siege of grief from her,
Betrothed and would have married her perforce
To County Paris. Then comes she to me,
And with wild looks bid me devise some mean
To rid her from this second marriage,
Or in my cell there would she kill herself.
Then gave I her (so tutored by my art)
A sleeping potion, which so took effect
As I intended, for it wrought on her
The form of death. Mean time I writ to Romeo
That he should hither come as this dire night

	To help to take her from her borrowed grave,

PRINCE

To help to take her from her borrowed grave,
Being the time the potion's force should cease.
But he which bore my letter, Friar John,
Was stayed by accident, and yesternight
Returned my letter back. Then all alone,
At the prefixèd hour of her waking,
Came I to take her from her kindred's vault,
Meaning to keep her closely at my cell,
Till I conveniently could send to Romeo.
But when I came, some minute ere the time
Of her awakening, here untimely lay
The noble Paris and true Romeo dead.
She wakes, and I entreated her come forth
And bear this work of heaven with patience.
But then a noise did scare me from the tomb,
And she too desperate would not go with me,
But as it seems, did violence on herself.

PRINCE

A glooming peace this morning with it brings,
The sun for sorrow will not show his head.
Go hence to have more talk of these sad things;
Some shall be pardoned, and some punishèd:
For never was a story of more woe
Than this of Juliet and her Romeo.

❋ *Building the play*

You are now going to build a play from the workshop explorations. Look back over the work that you have done. Make decisions about the scenes that could be incorporated in your play. These scenes include:

- freeze frames – feud
- improvisation – aftermath of feud
- improvisation – marriage
- speaking diary – prospective husband
- improvisation – love affairs
- depictions – masked ball
- dance – Romeo and Juliet
- duologue – balcony scene
- movement – lovers' partings
- scene – marriage
- slow motion sculptures – fight
- duologues – split stage
- duologue – Romeo and Juliet

- scene – marriage
- depiction – obedient Juliet
- chorus/monologue – Juliet discovered
- movement – funeral procession
- duologue – Romeo's news
- freeze frames – the tomb
- monologues.

Casting

You will need to cast the roles for the characters included in the scenes you have selected.

Linking the scenes

Consider whether any links other than the music are necessary between the scenes.

Rehearsing

Consider any changes or adjustments to the scenes that you may need to make to fit the performance space.

Performing

When you have thoroughly rehearsed the play, present it to an audience and encourage the audience to give you feedback on their responses to the play.

You may wish to develop a printed program that provides your audience with information that you have explored throughout the playbuilding process.

Write your own responses to the play and the playbuilding process that you have gone through in your journal. Keep a copy of the final script that you used for your performance.

When you have presented your version of the story, you may wish to explore the rest of Shakespeare's play, *Romeo and Juliet*.

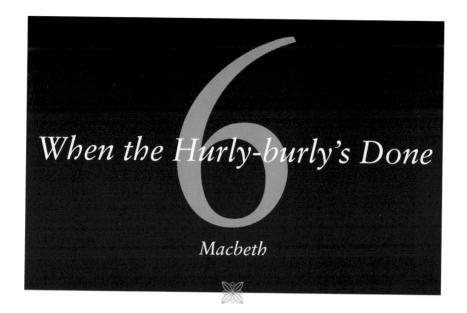

When the Hurly-burly's Done

Macbeth

In this unit of work you are going to explore the story of *Macbeth*. This story involves supernatural forces which may seem at first to be somewhat far-fetched in today's world. In this story, witches predict future events which come to pass, but they do not predict *how* these events will come to pass. Part of the interest of the story arises from the effects of these predictions on Macbeth and on his wife, Lady Macbeth.

✻ *Preliminary discussion*

Work with a small group. Talk about predicting the future, both in an historical context and in contemporary society. Who predicts the future?

Talk about the prophets of the Old Testament in the Christian Bible, and the fortune tellers that appear in many stories. You may wish to do some research to find out more about the kinds of predictions that these people made about the future.

What kinds of predictions do people make today? Think about such things as tarot cards, astrology, numerology and clairvoyants. You may wish to research how people predict the future from such things as the stars, numbers or from tarot cards.

Talk about how predictions might affect people. If something is predicted as going to happen to someone, does that person need to take any action, or feel any responsibility for the actions? How would it affect you? Would you want to know about something bad that was going to happen?

Imagine that a clairvoyant has predicted that you will receive some great reward. How would you feel? Imagine that a clairvoyant has predicted some potentially disastrous event in your life. How would you feel?

Write your ideas and feelings in your logbook.

✳ *When the hurly-burly's done*

The play that you are going to build involves the idea of witches who are predicting or perhaps controlling events in people's lives. Do you think that people who predict future happenings have control over these happenings?

Work with a small group and talk about the idea of witches. Do they exist? Or are they a figment of people's imagination used to explain otherwise inexplicable events?

Look at the drawing of the witch. The witch is presented as an old, ugly hag. This is a common stereotype of witches. Why do you think this stereotype exists? What ideas are associated with witches?

Are there other possible images of witches? Work with a small group. Create a sculpture that depicts your idea of witches. Try to work beyond the stereotype of the bent old woman.

Show your sculpture to the rest of the class. As you watch each group present their sculpture, suggest captions for each one that encapsulates the main idea of each image.

Record your ideas in your logbook.

✳ *You should be women*

Later in the play, *Macbeth*, Banquo describes the witches in these words:

> So withered and so wild in their attire,
> That look not like th'inhabitants o'th'earth,
> And yet are on't.

He then addresses the witches in these words:

> You seem to understand me,
> By each at once her choppy finger laying
> Upon her skinny lips; you should be women
> And yet your beards forbid me to interpret
> That you are so.

Spend some time discussing the images and ideas about witches that have been presented here. Imagine that you are the costume designer for a production of this play. Sketch the costumes and make-up you would use for the witches.

Record your ideas in your logbook.

✳ *I come, Graymalkin*

Today, we often associate witches with black cats. This image probably derives from the belief that witches used to have a 'familiar' demon spirit, usually in the form of an animal or a bird. The witches in *Macbeth* each have a 'familiar' demon.

The first witch has a grey cat called Graymalkin. The second witch has a toad called Paddock. The audience is not told what the third witch's demon spirit is. Later in the play, we learn that the third witch's familiar is called Harpier.

Work in groups of six. Talk about what kind of familiar or demon the third witch might have. Draw a sketch of the grey cat, the toad and the third familiar.

Each member of the group should take on the role of one of the witches or one of the familiars.

Improvise a series of scenes between each of the witches and the familiars. You may wish to give the familiars the powers of speech, or you may wish them to use sounds only. Experiment with different ways of doing this.

Spend some time talking about the ways that these characters interacted. What kind of relationship was created between each witch and the familiar?

Write your ideas in your logbook.

❋ *I come, Graymalkin. Paddock calls.*

Macbeth opens with a scene involving the three witches. They have been doing something, presumably evil, and are about to leave. The play opens with what is effectively the end of their activity, so the audience is left wondering what they have been up to.

Continue to work in your group of six with the roles of the familiars and the witches. Improvise a scene between the three witches and the three familiars.

When you have experimented with your scene, imagine that the three demons or familiars are anxious to depart and the three witches are lingering over the work that they have been doing. Create a scene in which the demons are trying to call their witches to come.

Show your improvised scenes to others in the class. Spend some time talking about these scenes.

Record your improvised scene in your logbook.

❋ *When the battle's lost, and won*

Continue to work in your group of six. Read through the opening scene of *Macbeth*, printed below. Talk about what the witches might be doing while they are saying these words. Talk about where the familiars might be – on the stage or already gone. Discuss the kinds of calls that each would be making to their witches.

FIRST WITCH	When shall we three meet again? In thunder, lightning, or in rain?
SECOND WITCH	When the hurly-burly's done, When the battle's lost, and won.
THIRD WITCH	That will be ere the set of sun.
FIRST WITCH	Where the place?
SECOND WITCH	Upon the heath.
THIRD WITCH	There to meet with Macbeth.
FIRST WITCH	I come, Graymalkin.
SECOND WITCH	Paddock calls.
THIRD WITCH	Anon.
ALL	Fair is foul, and foul is fair, Hover through the fog and filthy air.

Rehearse this scene, drawing on your improvisations involving the familiars and the witches. When you are satisfied with your scene, present it to the rest of the class.

Spend time discussing the scenes and the ideas that are created. Record your information in your logbook.

✳ Thane of Glamis

Macbeth is set in Scotland. It involves Scottish lords and their internal battles. The king is attempting to hold the country together. Duncan is the King of Scotland and his lords include Macbeth and Banquo. Both Macbeth and Banquo are loyal, brave, courageous soldiers who support the king against the rebels, fighting unceasingly in the battles in the war-torn country. But there are other lords who are rebels and who are fighting battles over the countryside.

Do some research about Scotland. Try to find pictures that show how these battles might have been fought during this period of history. What kinds of weapons were used?

Record your ideas in your logbook.

✳ Brave Macbeth

Work with a large group. Establish a series of freeze frames to depict the battles. In your frames show the loyalty of Macbeth and Duncan, and the rebels who are overcome by these brave soldiers. You may wish to create three to five frames, each one showing the progress of the battle and the fierceness of the fighting.

Show your freeze frames to other groups in the class. Talk about the images you have created and the ideas that are suggested by them.

Write a description of the images in your logbook. Record the ideas that arose from these.

✳ What bloody man is that?

The battles were occurring in different parts of the countryside in Scotland. Reporting what happened in one part of the country was an important aspect of the battle. The following edited version of a speech from *Macbeth* tells about one of the battles being fought.

Work with a small group. Read through this speech together and talk about the way that the Captain presents the events.

Select a section of the speech and create, in slow motion sculptures, the action that is being described in this section. You may wish to allocate a different section to each group.

CAPTAIN   The Merciless Macdonald –
Worthy to be a rebel, for to that
The multiplying villainies of nature
Do swarm upon him – from the Western Isles
Of kerns and galloglasses is supplied,
And Fortune on his damnèd quarrel smiling,
Showed like a rebel's whore.

                                 But all's too weak,
For brave Macbeth – well he deserves that name –
Disdaining Fortune, with his brandished steel
Which smoked with bloody execution,
Like Valour's minion carved out his passage
Till he faced the slave,
Which ne'er shook hands, nor bade farewell to him,
Till he unseamed him from the nave to th'chaps
And fixed his head upon our battlements.

As whence the sun 'gins his reflection,
Shipwrecking storms and direful thunders,
So from that spring whence comfort seemed to come,
Discomfort swells.
No sooner justice had, with valour armed,
Compelled these skipping kerns to trust their heels,
But the Norwegian lord, surveying vantage,
With furbished arms and new supplies of men
Began a fresh assault.

DUNCAN   Dismayed not this our captains, Macbeth and Banquo?

CAPTAIN   Yes, as sparrows, eagles, or the hare, the lion.
If I say sooth, I must report they were
As cannons over-charged with double cracks;
So they doubly redoubled strokes upon the foe.
Except they meant to bathe in reeking wounds
Or memorise another Golgotha.

...the Norwegian banners flout the sky
And fan our people cold.
Norway himself, with terrible numbers,
Assisted by that most disloyal traitor,
The Thane of Cawdor, began a dismal conflict,
Till that Bellona's bridegroom, lapped in proof,
Confronted him with self-comparisons,
Point against point, rebellious arm 'gainst arm,

Curbing his lavish spirit. And to conclude,
The victory fell on us.

When you are satisfied with your slow motion sculptures, rehearse them using some of the lines from the speech as a voice-over to the slow motion sculptures. You may wish to cut lines from the text.

Present the slow motion sculptures with the voice-over to the rest of the class. You may wish to have the groups present these sections in the order in which they occur, so that you can see the sequence of the battle.

Talk about the issues that the reporting of the battle scenes raise. Write your ideas in your logbook.

Record the script for this scene in your logbook.

⊛ *With his former title greet Macbeth*

The Thane of Cawdor is conquered and, as all traitors in those days, is immediately put to death. The common practice in Britain at this time was to behead the traitor and to mount his head on a pole and place this at the entrance to London Bridge.

Duncan, in giving out this punishment, speaks these lines:

No more that Thane of Cawdor shall deceive
Our bosom interest. Go pronounce his present death
And with his former title greet Macbeth.

Work with a small group and speak these lines as you think Duncan would have said them. Try various ways until you are satisfied with the sounds of the words and the rhythm and pace of the lines.

Now, create two depictions: one depiction should show the taking away of the title from the Thane of Cawdor and the other should show the execution of the Thane of Cawdor. How is he executed? You will need to decide what symbol you will use for the title – perhaps a coronet?

Record your ideas in your logbook.

✻ *Macbeth hath won*

Duncan also speaks this line as the final line of this scene in the play.

What he hath lost, noble Macbeth hath won.

Work with a small group. Experiment with ways of creating a chorus effect with this line. For instance, you may wish to have one member of the group say the line with others repeating or echoing the words lost and won. You will probably remember that these are the words which the witches spoke in the first scene of the play. You may wish to experiment with inserting these lines with the witches' lines to create a kind of echo.

Record your explorations and discoveries in your logbook.

✻ *Homeward he did come*

In the next scene the witches confront Macbeth with the predictions which will eventually drive him to his destruction. But first they celebrate their own powers as the first witch tells the story of the sailor's wife who annoyed her.

Work in groups and read through this scene. Try reading aloud, and let the words direct your voice. Don't try to put on a witch's voice, but try to find the voice within the lines.

FIRST WITCH	Where hast thou been, sister?
SECOND WITCH	Killing swine.
THIRD WITCH	Sister, where thou?
FIRST WITCH	A sailor's wife had chestnuts in her lap
	And munched, and munched, and munched. 'Give me', quoth I.
	'Aroint thee, witch', the rump-fed ronyon cries.
	Her husband's to Aleppo gone, master o'th'Tiger:
	But in a sieve I'll thither sail,
	And like a rat without a tail,
	I'll do, I'll do and I'll do.
SECOND WITCH	I'll give thee a wind.
FIRST WITCH	Thou'rt kind.

THIRD WITCH	And I another.
FIRST WITCH	I myself have all the other,
	And the very ports they blow,
	All the quarters that they know
	I'th'shipman's card.
	I'll drain him dry as hay:
	Sleep shall neither night nor day
	Hang upon his penthouse lid;
	He shall live a man forbid.
	Weary sennights nine times nine,
	Shall he dwindle, peak, and pine.
	Though his bark cannot be lost,
	Yet it shall be tempest-tossed.
	Look what I have.
SECOND WITCH	Show me, show me.
FIRST WITCH	Here I have a pilot's thumb,
	Wrecked as homeward he did come.

This scene shows the incredible power of the witches.

Improvise the scene between the sailor's wife and the first witch. Show your improvisations to other groups. Why do you think the first witch wants to take such strong revenge for this insult? What does this story have to do with the story of Macbeth?

When you have read through and are happy with the voices, experiment with creating the scene on the stage. Are the familiars involved in this scene? How does the actor playing the first witch actually get hold of the 'pilot's thumb'? When you have rehearsed this scene, show it to other groups in the class.

Record your explorations in your logbook.

✳ *Macbeth doth come*

The witches have the power to stir the elements. They create a spell for the arrival of Macbeth and Banquo.

Work in small groups. Read through the lines that they speak as they create the spell. Try to work out how they could say these lines so that a magical and evil atmosphere is created. Are the familiars on the stage during this scene? Does this scene benefit from music? What kinds of movements are suggested by the words?

THIRD WITCH	A drum, a drum;
	Macbeth doth come.
ALL	The weïrd sisters, hand in hand,
	Posters of the sea and land,

Thus do go, about, about,
Thrice to thine, and thrice to mine,
And thrice again, to make up nine.
Peace, the charm's wound up.

When you have rehearsed your scene, show it to the rest of the class. Talk about the features that help to create the mood of the scene.
Record your explorations in your logbook.

❈ So foul and fair a day

When Macbeth, the Thane of Glamis, meets the witches for the first time, he is returning with Banquo from their battle successes. The foul weather has, of course, been further stirred up by the witches' spell.

The witches know that Macbeth is coming and they are privileged to know what is to occur for Macbeth. But neither Macbeth nor Banquo are expecting this meeting or the information which the witches give them.

Replay the spell scene and as this scene ends have Macbeth and Banquo enter. Improvise what happens in the next moment in the scene.

Show your improvisations to others in the class. Spend some time in discussing the responses that the characters of Banquo and Macbeth made to the witches.

Record your improvisations in your logbook.

❈ Speak if you can

Work in groups. You will need at least five in each group – more if you decide that the familiars are also in the scene.

Read through the scene where the witches present the immediate prophecies to Banquo and Macbeth.

MACBETH   Speak if you can: what are you?

FIRST WITCH   All hail Macbeth, hail to thee, Thane of Glamis.

SECOND WITCH   All hail Macbeth, hail to thee, Thane of Cawdor.

THIRD WITCH   All hail Macbeth, that shalt be king hereafter.

BANQUO   Good sir, why do you start and seem to fear
               Things that do sound so fair? – I'th'name of truth
               Are ye fantastical, or that indeed
               Which outwardly ye show? My noble partner
               You greet with present grace and great prediction

Of noble having and of royal hope
That he seems rapt withal. To me you speak not.
If you can look into the seeds of time
And say which grain will grow and which will not,
Speak then to me, who neither beg nor fear
Your favours nor your hate.

FIRST WITCH	Hail.
SECOND WITCH	Hail.
THIRD WITCH	Hail.
FIRST WITCH	Lesser than Macbeth, and greater.
SECOND WITCH	Not so happy, yet much happier.
THIRD WITCH	Thou shalt get kings, though thou be none. So all hail Macbeth and Banquo.
FIRST WITCH	Banquo and Macbeth, all hail.
MACBETH	Stay, you imperfect speakers. Tell me more. By Sinel's death, I know I am Thane of Glamis, But how of Cawdor? The Thane of Cawdor lives A prosperous gentleman, and to be king Stands not within the prospect of belief, No more than to be Cawdor. Say from whence You owe this strange intelligence, or why Upon this blasted heath you stop our way With such prophetic greeting? Speak, I charge you.
BANQUO	The earth hath bubbles, as the water has, And these are of them. Whither are they vanished?
MACBETH	Into the air, and what seemed corporal, Melted, as breath into the wind. Would they had stayed.

Spend some time talking about why you think Macbeth is so stunned. Why is it Banquo who first questions the witches? Why does Macbeth wish they had stayed?

Spend some time rehearsing this scene. You will need to experiment with how the witches are to disappear.

Record your discoveries in your logbook.

✳ *Greet Macbeth*

Return to the scene where Duncan pronounces the death of Cawdor. The lines he spoke are repeated below.

No more that Thane of Cawdor shall deceive
Our bosom interest. Go pronounce his present death
And with his former title greet Macbeth.

Work with these lines again, but this time add a further depiction – the greeting of Macbeth with the title Thane of Cawdor. You should use the same symbol that you used in the earlier scene.

Place Banquo in this depiction. Now develop a scene using the words that Duncan spoke as a voice-over, and using the following dialogue. You will need to consider the ritualistic elements of some of these lines.

ANGUS   We are sent
                To give thee from our royal master thanks.

ROSS   And for an earnest of a great honour,
                He bade me, from him, call thee Thane of Cawdor.

Record your explorations in your logbook.

❋ *Two truths*

In many of Shakespeare's plays the characters speak directly to the audience. Imagine that following this scene, Banquo speaks to the audience. The other characters, including Macbeth, cannot hear what he is saying.

Work in a group. Play the scene with the bestowing of the title on Macbeth, then freeze the characters on the stage and allow Banquo to improvise a soliloquy to the audience where he tells them what he is thinking and feeling about this event.

Share your scenes with other groups in the class. Spend some time talking about Banquo's reaction to the events and to Macbeth.

Record your ideas in your logbook.

❋ *Chance may crown me*

Shakespeare gives Macbeth a monologue which he speaks while the other characters are on the stage. They cannot hear it, but they do observe and comment on how Macbeth is behaving – 'rapt'!

Work in groups of four. Explore this edited version of the speech, with one person taking on the words of Macbeth and the others taking on the roles of the witches and echoing words from their earlier scene. You may wish to consider which of the words would be most suitable for different sections of the speech – All hail Macbeth / hail to thee / Thane of Glamis / Thane of Cawdor / king hereafter.

MACBETH   Two truths are told,
                As happy prologues to the swelling act
                Of the imperial theme –
                This supernatural soliciting

Cannot be ill, cannot be good. If ill,
Why hath it given me earnest of success,
Commencing in a truth? I am Thane of Cawdor.
If good, why do I yield to that suggestion,
Whose horrid image doth unfix my hair
And makes my seated heart knock at my ribs
Against the use of nature? Present fears
Are less than horrible imaginings.
My thought, whose murder yet is but fantastical,
Shakes so my single state of man that function
Is smothered in surmise, and nothing is,
But what is not.
If chance will have me king, why chance may crown me
Without my stir.

Come what come may,
Time and the hour runs through the roughest day.

Talk about the thoughts running through Macbeth's mind. Think about how this could be conveyed to the audience through gesture or movement.

Rehearse this speech so that the witches' lines and movements act as a counterpointed chorus to Macbeth's lines.

Record your explorations and discoveries in your logbook.

✳ *In the day of my success*

Macbeth writes a letter to his wife telling her about the meeting with the witches. In the play, Lady Macbeth reads part of this letter aloud to the audience. The reading of a letter on the stage is another way in which the audience can learn about characters' thoughts. Sometimes we see a character writing the letter and at other times we see a character reading the letter. It is also possible to see both characters at the same time. We then have a view of their reactions and their relationships with one another.

Work with a partner. One of you should play Macbeth and one should play Lady Macbeth. Experiment with the writing/reading of this letter. You may wish to have Macbeth writing the letter and showing his reaction to what he is communicating to his wife, and then reverse the situation so that the audience can see her reaction. You could also experiment with a cross-over in the middle of the letter, so that Lady Macbeth takes over the reading of the letter after Macbeth has begun it.

Show your experiments to other groups and discuss what these different scenes show about the conspiracy that is established between the two characters.

'They met me in the day of success, and I have learned by the perfectest report they have more in them than mortal knowledge. When I burned in desire to question them further, they made themselves air, into which they vanished. Whiles I stood rapt in the wonder of it, came missives from the king who all-hailed me Thane of Cawdor, by which title before these weïrd sisters saluted me and referred me to the coming on of time, with "Hail, king that shalt be." This have I thought good to deliver thee, my dearest partner of greatness, that thou mightst not lose the dues of rejoicing by being ignorant of what greatness is promised thee. Lay it to thy heart and farewell.'

Record your ideas in your logbook.

✻ My dearest love

We see Lady Macbeth and Macbeth at various stages in the early part of the play. In their relationship we see the tensions that sometimes occur between husband and wife, but we also see the wife who totally supports and spurs her husband on to achieve his ambition.

Work with a partner to create a series of depictions which show moments of tension and tenderness between these two characters.

Read the following lines and select some to incorporate within the depictions that you create.

LADY MACBETH
        Great Glamis, worthy Cawdor,
    Greater than both by the all-hail hereafter.

MACBETH
        My dearest love.

MACBETH   We will speak further.

LADY MACBETH
        Only look up clear;
   To alter favour ever is to fear.
   Leave all the rest to me.

MACBETH   I dare do all that may become a man;
   Who dares do more is none.

LADY MACBETH
       What beast was't then
   That made you break this enterprise to me?

MACBETH   If we should fail?

LADY MACBETH   We fail?
   But screw your courage to the sticking-place,
   And we'll not fail.

MACBETH   This is a sorry sight.

LADY MACBETH   A foolish thought, to say a sorry sight.

| LADY MACBETH | Why did you bring these daggers from the place? They must lie there. Go carry them and smear The sleepy grooms with blood. |
| MACBETH | I'll go no more. I am afraid to think what I have done; Look on't again, I dare not. |

Record your ideas in your logbook.

✻ *The king's abed*

Duncan visits Macbeth's castle and after a very good party with plenty of wine the king retires to bed. Banquo has not yet retired to bed and Macbeth is waiting for everyone to go to bed so that he can enter Duncan's chamber to murder him, and then become king himself.

Work with a partner and improvise a scene which might take place between these two characters, Banquo and Macbeth, at this point.

Show your improvisations to another pair. Talk about the scenes and how the characters might be feeling.

Now work in groups of four and use the alter ego exercise (for more information, see chapter 1) to explore the innermost feelings and thoughts of these two characters. One person takes the role of Banquo and another is Banquo's alter ego. One person takes the role of Macbeth and another is Macbeth's alter ego.

After each line that Banquo or Macbeth speaks, their alter egos comment on how they are really feeling.

When you have had time to experiment with this exercise, try to tighten up the dialogue so that you can present the scene to the rest of the class.

Spend some time discussing the views of the characters portrayed in these scenes.

Record your ideas in your logbook.

✻ *Grace is dead*

The murder of Duncan is carried out by Macbeth, with assistance and support from his wife. The murdered body is discovered by Macduff, when he and other Thanes arrive at the castle early in the morning. In the process of the discovery, Macbeth murders the servants who were supposed to be guarding the king. Their hands had been smeared with blood by Lady Macbeth after the murder to make it seem that they were the guilty ones. As Macduff rings the alarm bells, people come on to the stage and are told of the death of the king.

Work in a large group. You are going to set up a series of freeze frames that show the stages in the discovery of the murder. For each frame, one character will speak a line or lines and the other characters will show their reactions.

Frame 1: Macbeth, Lennox, Macduff

MACDUFF O horror, horror, horror,
Tongue nor heart cannot conceive, nor name thee.

Frame 2: Macbeth, Lady Macbeth, Lennox, Macduff, Banquo

MACDUFF Our royal master's murdered.

Frame 3: Macbeth, Lady Macbeth, Lennox, Macduff, Banquo, Donaldbain, Malcolm

MACDUFF Your royal father's murdered.

Frame 4: Macbeth, Lady Macbeth, Lennox, Macduff, Banquo, Donaldbain, Malcolm

MACBETH Here lay Duncan,
His silver skin laced with golden blood
And his gashed stabs looked like a breach in nature,
For ruin's wasteful entrance.

Frame 5: Macbeth, Lady Macbeth, Lennox, Macduff, Banquo, Donaldbain, Malcolm

LADY MACBETH Help me hence, ho.

BANQUO Look to the lady.

Frame 6: Macbeth, Lennox, Macduff, Banquo, Donaldbain, Malcolm

BANQUO ...let us meet
And question this most bloody piece of work.

MACBETH Let's briefly put on manly readiness
And meet i'th'hall together.

Discuss the effects of the scene which has been created through these freeze frames.

Record this as a storyboard in your logbook.

✷ King, Cawdor, Glamis, all

The prophecies of the three witches have come true for Macbeth. Imagine that you are Banquo. How would you feel about the prophecies now?

Work in groups of four. Read the following edited version of the soliloquy that Banquo speaks at this point in the play, then rehearse this with a chorus using some of the witches lines from earlier in the play.

BANQUO   Thou hast it now, King, Cawdor, Glamis, all,
      As the weïrd women promised, and I fear
      Thou played'st most foully for't; yet it was said
      It should not stand in thy posterity,
      But that myself should be the root and father
      Of many kings. If there come truth from them –
      Why by the verities on thee made good,
      May they not be my oracles as well
      And set me up in hope?

Present your scene to the rest of the class. Why does Macbeth succumb to the witches while Banquo seems to be more immune to their evil?

✷ O full of scorpions is my mind

Macbeth admits to having terrible dreams which are tormenting his nightly sleep. Work in a small group. Talk about what these dreams might be about.

Read through some of the following words which Macbeth speaks, or which Lady Macbeth speaks to him or about him at different points in the play.

Use some of these words as the basis of a sound and movement collage that presents the bad dreams that Macbeth is experiencing.

• so foul and fair a day
• supernatural soliciting cannot be ill, cannot be good
• our duties are to your throne and state
• let not light see my black and deep desires
• look like th'innocent flower, but be the serpent under't
• we but teach bloody instruction
• he's here in double trust
• I have no spur to prick the sides of my intent
• vaulting ambition which o'erleaps itself
• art thou afeared
• I dare do all that may become a man
• screw your courage to the sticking-place
• I am settled
• false face must hide what the false heart doth know

- is this a dagger which I see before me
- art thou but a dagger of the mind
- on thy blade and dudgeon gouts of blood
- witchcraft celebrates pale Hecate's off'rings
- God bless us and amen
- sleep no more
- Macbeth shall sleep no more
- smear the sleepy grooms with blood
- the eye of childhood that fears a painted devil
- get on your night-gown
- 'twere best not know myself
- we have scorched the snake, not killed it.

You may wish to consider sounds as well as the lines of verse. Some of the sounds that are referred to in the play include:

- owl scream
- crickets cry
- knocking at the south entry
- bell
- death knell
- sounds of battle – swords etc.
- sounds of the alarm
- thunder, lightning etc.

Show your collage to other groups.
Record the outline of this collage in your logbook.

❈ Be innocent of the knowledge

In the earlier part of the play, Lady Macbeth has always been able to coax Macbeth out of his moments of doubt and despair, but as time goes on he shuts her out of his plans and his life.

Work with a partner. One of you take the part of Macbeth and the other of Lady Macbeth. Read through this scene. Try to find the sense of the relationship that now exists between these two characters. (Fleance is Banquo's son.)

MACBETH   Thou know'st that Banquo and his Fleance lives.

LADY MACBETH   But in them Nature's copy's not eterne.

MACBETH   There's comfort yet, they are assailable;
               Then be thou jocund: ere the bat hath flown
               His cloistered flight, ere to black Hecate's summons
               The shard-borne beetle with his drowsy hums

Hath rung night's yawning peal, there shall be done
A deed of dreadful note.

LADY MACBETH   What's to be done?

MACBETH   Be innocent of the knowledge, dearest chuck,
Till thou applaud the deed. Come, seeling night,
Scarf up the tender eye of pitiful day
And with thy bloody and invisible hand
Cancel and tear to pieces that great bond
Which keeps me pale. Light thickens,
And the crow makes wing to th'rooky wood;
Good things of day begin to droop and drowse,
Thou marvell'st at my words, but hold thee still;
Things bad begun, make strong themselves by ill.
So prithee, go with me.

The deed which Macbeth is referring to here is the imminent murder of Banquo and Fleance. He has engaged three murderers to do this job and a fourth murderer also arrives at the scene claiming to have been sent by Macbeth to join in the deed. You might want to question whether this murderer has, in fact, been sent by Macbeth.

Improvise the murder scene using slow motion sculptures. The characters are the four murderers, Banquo and Fleance. In the dark, Fleance escapes, but Banquo is murdered.

When you are satisfied with your improvised slow motion sculptures, present these as background to the scene with Macbeth and Lady Macbeth. Show your version of the scene to others in the class. Discuss the effects of this scene.

Record your ideas in your logbook.

✿ *Blood will have blood*

Following the murder of Banquo, Macbeth is holding a banquet for all the lords. The ghost of Banquo appears at this banquet and Macbeth is so shocked and disturbed that he is unable to keep his cool.

Work in a large group. Set up a scene at a banquet table. There should be one spare seat at this table. Improvise dialogue between the guests at the table. After Macbeth enters, he sees the ghost of Banquo sitting in his place. He speaks four times to the ghost in the scene. Each time he speaks, the ghost goes out again.

Below are the words that he speaks to the ghost on each of the occasions that the ghost returns to the table. Read these words, then improvise a scene at the banquet with Macbeth speaking to the ghost either using these words or improvised dialogue.

MACBETH   Thou canst not say I did it; never shake
                       Thy gory locks at me!

                       Why, what care I? If thou canst nod, speak too.
                       If charnel houses and our graves must send
                       Those that we bury back, our monuments
                       Shall be the maws of kites.

                       Avaunt and quit my sight! Let the earth hide thee!
                       Thy bones are marrowless, thy blood is cold;
                       Thou hast no speculation in those eyes
                       Which thou dost glare with.

                       What man dare, I dare;
                       Approach thou like the rugged Russian bear,
                       The armed rhinoceros, or th'Hyrcan tiger,
                       Take any shape but that, and my firm nerves
                       Shall never tremble. Or be alive again,
                       And dare me to the desert with thy sword;
                       If trembling I inhabit then, protest me
                       The baby of a girl. Hence horrible shadow,
                       Unreal mock'ry hence.

This scene is the last time that the audience sees Macbeth and Lady
Macbeth together. You may wish to consider how Lady Macbeth feels about
her husband's behaviour in this scene.
    Record the scene in your logbook.

✻ *Trade and traffic with Macbeth*

Hecate is the 'goddess' of witches. She enters the play at this point and
chastises the three witches for their work.
    The following lines are an edited version of her speech to the other three
witches. Read them and then create an improvisation using any of the lines
or words you wish. The sections signal stages which may help with the
improvisation.

HECATE   How did you dare
                       To trade and traffic with Macbeth
                       In riddles and affairs of death?
                       And I the mistress of your charms,
                       The close contriver of all harms,
                       Was never called to bear my part
                       Or show the glory of our art?

                       And which is worse, all you have done
                       Hath been but for a wayward son,

Spiteful and wrathful, who, as others do,
Loves for his own ends, not for you.

But make amends now. Get you gone,
And at the pit of Acheron
Meet me i'th'morning. Thither he
Will come to know his destiny.
Your vessels and your spells provide,
Your charms and everything beside.

Upon the corner of the moon
There hangs a vap'rous drop profound;
I'll catch it ere it come to ground;
And that distilled by magic sleights,
Shall raise such artificial sprites
As by the strength of their illusion
Shall draw him on to his confusion.

He shall spurn fate, scorn death, and bear
His hopes 'bove wisdom, grace, and fear.
And you all know, security
Is mortals' chiefest enemy.

Record your improvisation in your logbook.

✕ *Double, double toil and trouble*

The first part of the apparition scene deals with the witches and their hell broth.

Work in groups. Make a list of the things that the witches throw into the cauldron.

FIRST WITCH	Thrice the brindled cat hath mewed.
SECOND WITCH	Thrice and once the hedge-pig whined.
THIRD WITCH	Harpier cries, ''Tis time, 'tis time.'
FIRST WITCH	Round about the cauldron go;
	In the poisoned entrails throw.
	Toad, that under cold stone
	Days and nights has thirty-one
	Sweltered venom sleeping got,
	Boil thou first i'th'charmèd pot.
ALL	Double, double toil and trouble;
	Fire burn, and cauldron bubble.
SECOND WITCH	Fillet of a fenny snake,
	In the cauldron boil and bake:

	Eye of newt, and toe of frog,
	Wool of bat, and tongue of dog,
	Adder's fork, and blind-worm's sting,
	Lizard's leg, and howlet's wing,
	For a charm of powerful trouble,
	Like a hell-broth, boil and bubble.
ALL	Double, double toil and trouble;
	Fire burn, and cauldron bubble.
THIRD WITCH	Scale of dragon, tooth of wolf,
	Witches' mummy, maw and gulf
	Of the ravined salt-sea shark,
	Root of hemlock, digged i'th'dark;
	Liver of blaspheming Jew,
	Gall of goat, and slips of yew,
	Slivered in the moon's eclipse;
	Nose of Turk, and Tartar's lips,
	Finger of birth-strangled babe,
	Ditch-delivered by a drab,
	Make the gruel thick and slab.
	Add thereto a tiger's chawdron
	For th'ingredience of our cauldron.

Imagine that you are the set and props designer for the play. Make sketches of the cauldron and the objects that are to be thrown into it. You may wish to consider how these could be made, or what substitute objects could be used. Sketch how the stage would look for this scene.

✳ *Like elves and fairies in a ring*

After Hecate arrives, the four witches dance like elves and fairies in a ring.

HECATE	O well done! I commend your pains,
	And every one shall share i'th'gains;
	And now about the cauldron sing
	Like elves and fairies in a ring,
	Enchanting all that you put in.

Talk about why Shakespeare has used that reference. What type of dance would you use? What effect might this have on the audience, watching witches dancing around a cauldron like elves and fairies?

Work in groups of four to choreograph a suitable dance.

Show your version of the dance to other groups. Discuss the effects of these dances on the audience.

Record your dance in your logbook.

※ *A deed without a name*

The apparition scene is one of the most powerful scenes in this play. The predictions which Hecate has made about Macbeth's behaviour all come true. He has become so overconfident that he fails to hear the full impact of the prophecies, and when the apparitions appear, his obsession with knowing the future clouds his vision.

The apparitions consist of an armed head, a bloody child, a crowned child with a tree in his hand, and a display of eight kings, the last with a glass in his hand and Banquo's ghost following him. These apparitions come from within the spell that the witches have created in the cauldron.

Work in small groups. Imagine that you are designers for a production of the play. Sketch the designs for each of these apparitions. You will need to consider how each one will appear. Will the witches hold them as they rise from the cauldron? Can they be puppets on sticks? This will have echoes for the audience from the Thane of Cawdor and the ending of *Macbeth*.

When you are satisfied with your sketches, make these props and then rehearse this edited version of the scene.

SECOND WITCH	By the pricking of my thumbs, Something wicked this way comes.
MACBETH	How now, you secret, black, and midnight hags! What is't you do?
ALL THE WITCHES	A deed without a name.
MACBETH	I conjure you by that which you profess, Howe'er you come to know it, answer me. ...answer me To what I ask you.
FIRST WITCH	Speak.
SECOND WITCH	Demand.
THIRD WITCH	We'll answer.
FIRST WITCH	Say, if thou'dst rather hear it from our mouths, Or from our masters?
MACBETH	Call 'em, let me see 'em. First witch Pour in sow's blood, that hath eaten Her nine farrow; grease that's sweaten From the murderer's gibbet throw Into the flame.
ALL THE WITCHES	Come high or low: Thyself and office deftly show.
MACBETH	Tell me, thou unknown power –

FIRST WITCH	He knows thy thought; Hear his speech, but say thou nought.
FIRST APPARITION	Macbeth, Macbeth, Macbeth: beware Macduff, Beware the Thane of Fife. Dismiss me. Enough.
MACBETH	Whate'er thou art, for thy good caution, thanks; Thou hast harped my fear aright. But one word more –
FIRST WITCH	He will not be commanded. Here's another, More potent than the first.
SECOND APPARITION	Macbeth, Macbeth, Macbeth.
MACBETH	Had I three ears, I'd hear thee.
SECOND APPARITION	Be bloody, bold, and resolute; laugh to scorn The power of man, for none of woman born Shall harm Macbeth.
MACBETH	Then live, Macduff, what need I fear of thee? But yet I'll make assurance double sure And take a bond of fate: thou shalt not live, That I may tell pale-hearted fear it lies, And sleep in spite of thunder. What is this, That rises like the issue of a king And wears upon his baby-brow the round And top of sovereignty?
ALL THE WITCHES	Listen, but speak not to 't.
THIRD APPARITION	Be lion-mettled, proud, and take no care Who chafes, who frets, or where conspirers are. Macbeth shall never vanquished be until Great Birnam Wood to high Dunsinane hill Shall come against him.
MACBETH	That will never be: Who can impress the forest, bid the tree Unfix his earthbound root? Sweet bodements, good. Rebellious dead, rise never till the wood Of Birnam rise, and our high-placed Macbeth Shall live the lease of nature, pay his breath To time and mortal custom. Yet my heart Throbs to know one thing. Tell me, if your art Can tell so much, shall Banquo's issue ever Reign in this kingdom?
ALL THE WITCHES	Seek to know no more.
MACBETH	I will be satisfied. Deny me this, And an eternal curse fall on you. Let me know.
FIRST WITCH	Show!
SECOND WITCH	Show!

THIRD WITCH	Show!
ALL THE WITCHES	Show his eyes and grieve his heart,
	Come like shadows, so depart.
MACBETH	Thou art too like the spirit of Banquo. Down!
	Thy crown does sear mine eyeballs. And thy hair,
	Thou other gold-bound brow, is like the first;
	A third, is like the former. – Filthy hags,
	Why do you show me this? – A fourth? Start, eyes!
	What, will the line stretch out to th'crack of doom?
	Another yet? A seventh? I'll see no more.
	And yet the eighth appears, who bears a glass
	Which shows me many more. And some I see,
	That two-fold balls and treble sceptres carry.
	Horrible sight! Now I see 'tis true,
	For the blood-boltered Banquo smiles upon me,
	And points at them for his. What, is this so?
FIRST WITCH	Ay, sir, all this is so. But why
	Stands Macbeth thus amazedly?
	Come, sisters, cheer we up his sprites,
	And show the best of our delights.
	I'll charm the air to give a sound,
	While you perform your antic round
	That this great king may kindly say,
	Our duties did his welcome pay.

Record your ideas in your logbook.

✳ *My dread exploits*

The show of kings snaps Macbeth into immediate action. He receives the news of Macduff's flight to England and immediately decides that he must wipe out the whole line of Macduff's family.

MACBETH	The castle of Macduff I will surprise;
	Seize upon Fife; give to th'edge o'th'sword
	His wife, his babes, and all unfortunate souls
	That trace him in his line.

Work in a small group. Have one person speak these lines of Macbeth. The rest of the group should set up a tableau of Macduff's family lined up behind Macbeth. One person should enter and cut down each of the family members as Macbeth speaks the line.

Record your ideas in your logbook.

✳ *A mind diseased*

Lady Macbeth is, by this stage, sorely troubled by the events and a great gulf appears to have opened up between Macbeth and Lady Macbeth.

Lady Macbeth has taken to walking in her sleep. She carries a lighted candle with her, and talks about some of the events that are troubling her.

The lines below are some of those which Lady Macbeth speaks as she walks in her sleep and tries to wash the blood from her hands in the flame of the candle. Work with a partner. Take some of these lines and experiment with the way that Lady Macbeth might say them.

> Yet here's a spot.

> Out damned spot! Out, I say!

> One, two. Why then 'tis time to do't. Hell is murky.

> Fie, my lord, fie, a soldier, and afeared? What need we fear? Who knows it, when none can call our power to account?

> Yet who would have thought the old man to have had so much blood in him?

> The Thane of Fife had a wife. Where is she now?

> What, will these hands ne'er be clean?

> No more o'that, my lord, no more o'that. You mar all with this starting.

> Here's the smell of the blood still; all the perfumes of Arabia will not sweeten this little hand. O, O, O.

> Wash your hands, put on your night-gown, look not so pale. I tell you again, Banquo's buried; he cannot come out on's grave.

> To bed, to bed; there's knocking at the gate. Come, come, come, come, give me your hand; what's done cannot be undone. To bed, to bed, to bed.

Write your impressions and ideas in your logbook.

✳ *Cure her of that*

A doctor who has been attending her has not been able to cure her of the pains of her diseased mind. Macbeth does not seem able to understand the depths of her suffering, until he finally learns of her death.

Work with a partner. Rehearse the two excerpts below, then play these moments on either side of the sleepwalking moments.

Excerpt 1

MACBETH   How does your patient, doctor?

DOCTOR   Not so sick, my lord,
         As she is troubled with thick-coming fancies
         That keep her from her rest.

MACBETH   Cure her of that.
         Canst thou not minister to a mind diseased,
         Pluck from the memory a rooted sorrow,
         Raze out the written troubles of the brain,
         And with some sweet oblivious antidote
         Cleanse the stuffed bosom of that perilous stuff
         Which weighs upon the heart?

DOCTOR   Therein the patient
         Must minister to himself.

Excerpt 2

MACBETH   What is that noise?

SEYTON   It is the cry of women, my good lord.

MACBETH   I have almost forgot the taste of fears;
         The time has been, my senses would have cooled
         To hear a night-shriek and my fell of hair
         Would at a dismal treatise rouse and stir
         As life were in't. I have supped full with horrors;
         Direness familiar to my slaughterous thoughts
         Cannot once start me. Wherefore was that cry?

SEYTON   The queen, my lord, is dead.

MACBETH   She should have died hereafter;
         There would have been a time for such a word.
         Tomorrow, and tomorrow, and tomorrow
         Creeps in this petty pace from day to day
         To the last syllable of recorded time;
         And all our yesterdays have lighted fools
         The way to dusty death. Out, out, brief candle,
         Life's but a walking shadow, a poor player
         That struts and frets his hour upon the stage
         And then is heard no more. It is a tale
         Told by an idiot, full of sound and fury
         Signifying nothing.

Record your ideas in your logbook.

❋ *Birnam Wood remove to Dunsinane*

Macbeth is confident that he is safe from harm until Birnam Wood moves to Dunsinane. He has not thought through ways in which this might happen. In fact the forces of Malcolm and the English have been harnessed and are moving towards Dunsinane. They cut branches from trees and use them as camouflage as they move to Dunsinane.

Set up this edited version of the scene with Macbeth in the centre of the performing space, representing his fortified castle Dunsinane. Surrounding him, advancing towards the castle are the soldiers, each one disguised behind the branch of a tree. He cannot hear or see them. Finally Macduff approaches and challenges Macbeth.

Choreograph a slow motion version of this scene.

MACBETH
Bring me no more reports, let them fly all;
Till Birnam Wood remove to Dunsinane,
I cannot taint with fear.
The spirits that know
All mortal consequences have pronounced me thus:
'Fear not, Macbeth, no man that's born of woman
Shall e'er have power upon thee.'
I will not be afraid of death and bane,
Till Birnam Forest come to Dunsinane.

MALCOLM
Let every soldier hew him down a bough,
And bear't before him; thereby shall we shadow
The numbers of our host and make discovery
Err in report of us.

MACBETH
Hang out our banners on the outward walls;
The cry is still, 'They come.' Our castle's strength
Will laugh a siege to scorn; here let them lie
Till famine and the ague eat them up.

MESSENGER
As I did stand my watch upon the hill
I looked toward Birnam and anon methought
The wood began to move.

MACBETH
                                   If thou speak'st false,
Upon the next tree shalt thou hang alive
Till famine cling thee.
I pull in resolution and begin
To doubt th'equivocation of the fiend
That lies like truth. 'Fear not, till Birnam Wood
Do come to Dunsinane', and now a wood
Comes toward Dunsinane. Arm, arm, and out!

If this which he avouches does appear,
There is nor flying hence nor tarrying here.
Ring the alarum bell! Blow wind, come wrack;
At least we'll die with harness on our back.

MALCOLM Now near enough; your leafy screens throw down
And show like those you are.

MACDUFF Make all our trumpets speak; give them all breath,
These clamorous harbingers of blood and death.

MACDUFF Turn, hell-hound, turn.

MACBETH Of all men else I have avoided thee.

MACDUFF My voice is in my sword, thou bloodier villain
Than terms can give thee out.

MACBETH   Thou losest labour.
As easy mayst thou the intrenchant air
With thy keen sword impress as make me bleed.
Let fall thy blade on vulnerable crests;
I bear a charmed life which must not yield
To one of woman born.

MACDUFF   Despair thy charm,
And let the angel whom thou still hast served
Tell thee, Macduff was from his mother's womb
Untimely ripped.

MACBETH Accursèd be that tongue that tells me so,
For it hath cowed my better part of man;
And be these juggling fiends no more believed
That palter with us in a double sense,
That keep the word of promise to our ear
And break it to our hope. I'll not fight with thee.

MACDUFF Then yield thee coward,
And live to be the show and gaze o'th'time.
We'll have thee, as our rarer monsters are,
Painted upon a pole and underwrit,
'Here may you see the tyrant.'

MACBETH   I will not yield
To kiss the ground before young Malcolm's feet
And to be baited with the rabble's curse.
Though Birnam Wood be come to Dunsinane
And thou opposed being of no woman born,
Yet I will try the last. Before my body,
I throw my warlike shield. Lay on, Macduff,
And damned be him that first cries, 'Hold, enough!'

Hail, King

The play ends with order restored and the rightful king on the throne. Macbeth's head has been cut off and placed on a pole. Read the following excerpt and use it as the basis of an improvised scene that could end the action of this play.

MACDUFF
Hail, King, for so thou art. Behold where stands
Th'usurper's cursèd head. The time is free.
Hail, King of Scotland.

MALCOLM
We shall not spend a large expense of time
Before we reckon with your several loves
And make us even with you.
What's more to do
As calling home our exiled friends abroad
That fled the snares of watchful tyranny,
Producing forth the cruel ministers
Of this dead butcher and his fiend-like queen.
So, thanks to all at once and to each one,
Whom we invite to see us crowned at Scone.

Building the play

Look back over your work. Reread your logbook entries. You are going to build a play that tells the story of Macbeth.

Select scenes which you wish to include in your play. These could include:

- improvisation – witches
- scene – witches
- freeze frames – battles
- slow motion sculptures – Macbeth's conquest
- depictions – Duncan's pronouncement
- chorus
- improvisations – witches' powers
- scene – spells and prophecies
- ritual – Macbeth's titles
- monologue – Banquo
- chorus
- split scene – Macbeth/Lady Macbeth
- alter ego
- freeze frames – murder
- soliloquy – Banquo

- sound and movement collage – Macbeth
- duologue – Macbeth/Lady Macbeth
- slow motion sculptures – Banquo's murder
- scene – banquet
- scene – witches
- dance – witches
- scene – apparitions
- tableau – Macduff
- scene – sleepwalking
- slow motion sculpture – Birnam Wood.

Casting

You will need to decide on actors for the roles that appear in the scenes you have included.

Rehearsing

Consider whether you will need to make any adjustments to the scenes. Rehearse the spacing and timing of each scene.

Linking the scenes

Consider whether any links other than music are necessary between the scenes.

Performing

When you have thoroughly rehearsed the play, present it to an audience and encourage the audience to give you feedback on their responses to the play.

You may wish to develop a printed program that provides your audience with information that you have explored throughout the playbuilding process.

Write your own responses to the play and the playbuilding process that you have gone through in your journal. Keep a copy of the final script that you used for your performance.

When you have presented your version of the story, you may wish to explore the rest of Shakespeare's play, *Macbeth*.

Epilogue

The following workshop activities and strategies have been used in this book.

Logbook

The logbook is an account of the explorations of the workshops. It enables an ongoing record of the activities, as well as an opportunity to record scenarios, scripts and character descriptions. It is a personal record for each student.

Sculptures

Sculptures are created using the bodies of actors to explore and establish the physical characteristics of characters.

Slow motion sculptures

Slow motion sculptures are sculptures which move in very slow motion, showing the particular physical characteristics of the particular character.

Depictions

Depictions are three-dimensional images created primarily with the bodies of the actors, but may also use furniture and props. These may also be photographed, or may be drawn as a cartoon version or a storyboard script. Depictions are also called still images, still photographs or tableaux.

Captioned depictions

The workshop audience of a depiction respond to the depiction by providing a caption for the image that they see.

Speech balloon depictions

The workshop audience of a depiction may provide lines for characters in a depiction. These are given in the form of speech balloons. The depiction may be replayed with the speech balloons spoken out loud to other characters.

Thought balloon depictions

The workshop audience of a depiction may provide the inner thoughts for characters in a depiction. The depiction may be replayed with the thought balloons spoken out loud in the form of asides to the audience.

Freeze frames

Freeze frames comprise a series of linked depictions which show the progress of a particular line of action. When freeze frames are shown to a workshop audience, the audience close their eyes as each frame is set up and open them to view each successive frame, thereby creating a shutter effect.

Freeze-dissolve-freeze

Freeze-dissolve-freeze is a technique in which each freeze frame is linked by a slow motion sculpture.

Improvisation

Improvisation involves the creation of scenes, working spontaneously. The improvisation may be dramatically structured in some way. Improvisation may be based on the reading of a scene which is then spontaneously re-enacted.

Collage

This device is linked to the notion of collage in the visual arts. It consists of a compilation of images that make up a whole statement.

Sound collage

This is a collage that is made with sound. It may consist of music, sounds, vocal sounds and/or words. It is sometimes also referred to as a soundscape.

Movement collage

This is a collage that is made with movement. The movement may have a ritualised quality. It may also make use of sound.

Dumbshow

Dumbshow is a type of scene which is enacted without words. It is similar to mime although it may use signalling, and may also make use of props and furniture, while mime tends not to use these.

Alter ego

Alter ego is a technique in which the inner thoughts of a character are revealed through the physical representation on the stage of the character's other self. The alter ego usually stands behind the real character and speaks after that character has spoken, revealing those inner thoughts and feelings to the audience.

Inner thoughts chorus

This is similar to the alter ego except that here a chorus of people represent the inner thoughts. Usually the character stands in the middle with the chorus surrounding him or her. The character usually begins and ends the scene with the inner thoughts expressing the character's conflicting emotions and moving around the character.

Speaking diary

Speaking diary is another way in which a character may reveal inner thoughts. Here the character is speaking aloud the thoughts that are being recorded in a diary. This technique can also be used to reveal the contents of letters.

Voice-over

Voice-over is another technique which can be used to explore inner thoughts. Here the voice is either pre-recorded, or spoken by an offstage actor, while the character performs some action on the stage.

Intercutting scene/split scene

In this technique, two similar or contrasting actions occur simultaneously, or in succession on the stage. Sometimes the lines of each scene will be intersecting or intercutting.

Hot seat

Hot seat involves a character being interrogated as to motives for actions. The interrogators may be in a variety of roles, both within the play and outside the play.